# Paint It!

## 35+
**Dynamic Weekend Decorative Paint Projects**

Irene Mumby

Mumby & Associates Limited

First published in 1999 by
Mumby & Associates Limited
7040 Financial Drive
Mississauga, Ontario
L5N 7H5


ISBN  0-9684723-0-3



Produced by
Publications-Plus Inc.
2330 Millrace Court, Unit 2
Mississauga, Ontario
L5N 1W2

Printed and bound in Canada

Book Design:      Derek Chung
Photography:      Al Peacock
Project Manager:  Judith Romagnolo
Styling:          Suzanne Davison Interior Designs Inc.

*Although all possible measures have been taken to ensure the accuracy of the material presented, neither the author nor the publishers are liable in case of misinterpretation of directions or misapplication.*

# Acknowledgements

*PAINT IT!* could not have happened without the creative input of the many talented people whose projects appear on the pages of this book. No less important to the book's production are those, who contributed support, advice and encouragement throughout the project. It is my pleasure to express my thanks and gratitude to all these colleagues and friends.

My warmest thanks to everybody at Mumby & Associates Limited for their limitless dedication and hard work — especially to Judith Romagnolo, who spearheaded production and assisted in creating many projects; and to Pooran Bishram and Tom Widdes for their technical expertise and eagle eyes. I am grateful to all the suppliers whose products made the projects possible: *Dynamic, The Flood Paint Specialty Company, Old Masters, Wm. Zinsser & Co., DecoArt, Symphony Art Inc., Buckingham Stencils, Blue Mountain Stencils, Crown, Paint Design, DCP-Lojha Inc., Tye-Sil, Hammerite, Whizz and Ritins.*

I thank my good friends Bonnie and Chuck Stewart for allowing us to paint their daughter Erinn's playhouse; and Trish and Mark Stevens for being so patient while we invaded their home with paint and cameras in hand.

Interior designer Suzanne Davison showed boundless enthusiasm and exemplary good taste in styling the projects for photography. Photographer Al Peacock diligently worked to capture the best possible images on film. And graphic designer Derek Chung used his creative talents to turn all the hard work into a beautiful book. I thank them warmly.

Finally, I am grateful to my biggest supporters — my husband, James, and my children, James and Jillian — who showed unlimited confidence and patience while I worked on this book.

Irene Mumby

# Contents

# Inspired interior projects

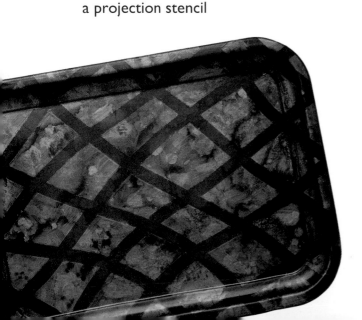

# Exciting exterior projects

# Products that make your projects look great

# Foreword

A vid do-it-yourselfers and passionate decorators all know how exciting it is to work at creative projects that rev up a room, brighten a home, add spice to interiors and put extra bloom in the garden. Look around at all the new hardware and home-dec stores sprouting in every neighborhood. They are overflowing with new — and irresistible — products. Check out video shops that rent how-to tapes. Tune in to television channels dedicated to home decorating that run around the clock. Everyone, it seems, is climbing onto the DIY (do-it-yourself) bandwagon.

The appeal of DIY decorating has many facets. Personal satisfaction underscored with pride probably tops the list: "I did it myself!" Conquering a challenge plays a part: "Can I *really* do this?" Necessity must not be overlooked.: "I need a new table/chair/lamp; it would be cheaper to do it myself." And recreation is often the motivator: "Okay, I paid $1 for this tray at a yard sale; let's see what I can do with it."

What about *you*? Are you looking for ideas to get you started on DIY projects for your home? If you are, you have come to the right place: *PAINT IT!* has more than 35 colorfully illustrated ideas to tempt your creativity. Each project is graded for its level of complexity, so that, novice or experienced, you can tell at a glance if you'll enjoy making it. All supplies are neatly listed to make shopping quick and easy. Complete instructions take you from start to finish every time. Finally, our product section outlines everything you need to know in order to choose the best materials for all the projects you may want to undertake.

When you have finished reading the book, I know you'll want to be part of the buzz that DIY decorating generates. So, climb on our bandwagon and have some fun! I guarantee you'll be pleased with the results.

**Complexity rating**

Before starting a project, check out the following symbols. They indicate the degree of expertise you need to succeed:

You're handy with tools.

You love making things but haven't done much in the past.

You would like to make something but have no previous experience.

# Inspired interior projects

Every home should reflect the personalities of the people who live in it. We all like to be surrounded by things we like, objects that make us comfortable or give us pleasure. The house that's filled with furnishings and decorations its occupants have created themselves is often the home in which visitors feel most comfortable, because it's so — well — *personal*.

Creating a happy pretty environment has never been easier. Fixing up flea-market or garage sale *finds* is now an international pastime. Ready-to-finish furniture built in myriad decorating styles makes it easy to put your personal stamp on a basic item so that you get *exactly* what you want. Quick-drying paints come in countless colors, finishes and textures.

Nobody can really tell you about the joy and satisfaction you'll feel when your handiwork is finished.

Look around your own house: do you see places you'd like to embellish or areas that could use another piece of furniture? Does your basement or attic harbor discarded items that you could pull out and work on? Chances are you've answered *yes*, so read on and be inspired! Your evenings and weekends are about to be filled with creative fun-to-do activities.

## WHAT YOU NEED

- a secretary-desk or other piece of furniture
- Dynamic Plastic Drop Cloth
- 180-grit sandpaper
- Dynamic Tack Cloth
- 4-inch Whizz Premium Fabric Roller and Tray Set
- 1 1-qt/946-mL can Zinsser Bulls Eye 1-2-3 Primer/Sealer
- 1 1-qt/946-mL can white flat latex paint
- 1 16-oz/473-mL bottle Decorative Glaze, *Mocha*
- Symphony 1-inch Grey Goat Hair Blender Brush
- 1 16-oz/473-mL bottle Decorative Glaze, *Golden Yellow*
- Dynamic ¾-inch All Purpose Brush
- DecoArt Easy Blend Stencil Paint: 1 1-oz/29.6-mL jar each of: *Snow White*; *Cadmium Yellow*; *Avocado Green*; *Forest Green*; *Ebony Black*; *Lavender*; *Williamsburg Blue*; *True Blue*; *Gooseberry Pink*
- 3 2-oz/59-mL bottles DecoArt Americana Acrylic Paint, *Sage Green*
- Buckingham Stencils: *Hanging Basket*; *Sword Fern*; *English Ivy*; *Blossoms*; *Berry Border*
- Buckingham ½-inch Stencil Brush
- Buckingham Stencil Adhesive Spray
- 1 1-qt/946-mL can Old Masters H₂0 Acrylic Polyurethane Interior Finish (*satin*)
- 400-grit sandpaper
- 2-inch Poly-Brush

# Renaissance Revival

*Resuscitate a discarded drop-front desk*

## WHAT TO DO

1. Place the desk on the drop cloth. Sand the desk thoroughly with 180-grit sandpaper, then wipe with the tack cloth to remove all particles.

2. Using the Whizz roller, apply 1 coat of primer/sealer. Let dry for 2 hours.

3. Apply 1 coat of white flat latex paint. Let dry.

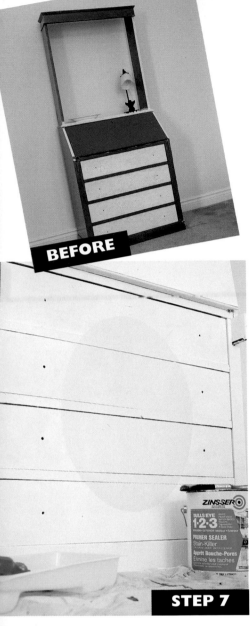

**BEFORE**

**STEP 7**

**STEP 11**

4. Mix about 1/4 cup of *Mocha* glaze with an equal amount of water. Using the blender brush, apply the mixture in light cloudy shapes over about a third of the surface. Mix more paint with water, as required.

5. Repeat, using *Golden Yellow* glaze mixed with equal parts water, covering the remaining area and overlapping the *Mocha*-glazed areas slightly.

6. Draw an oval on the front, as shown. (An oval picture frame makes a good pattern.)

7. Combine equal parts *Snow White* and *Cadmium Yellow* Easy Blend Stencil Paint. Using the 3/4-inch brush, paint inside the oval shape.

8. Paint the top and bottom trim and inside the desk, using 2 coats of Americana *Sage Green* paint and the 3/4-inch brush. Let dry and sand between coats, using 180-grit sandpaper, wiping clean with the tack cloth.

9. To stencil the main design, mark the positioning of the basket on the front: hold the *Hanging Basket* stencil in place and mark its outline with a pencil. Remove the stencil.

10. To create moss, use the stencil brush and *Avocado Green* stencil paint to *pounce* the paint over about 60 percent of the basket area, extending the paint slightly beyond the basket outline. Use *Forest Green* stencil paint and the stencil brush to fill in the remaining spaces, overlapping the first paint slightly.

11. Stencil the basket: spray the underside of the stencil with adhesive and press in place on the desk. Using the stencil brush and *Ebony Black* stencil paint, dab the brush over the stencil openings.

12. Add the leaves, using assorted stencils and *Avocado Green* and *Forest Green* stencil paints. Paint some darker than others; vary the shading.

13. Stencil in flowers, using yellow, blue and pink stencil paints and assorted stencils.

14. Stencil the border, using *Avocado Green* stencil paint and the *Berry Border* stencil. Stencil random flowers and leaves on the top and sides of the desk.

15. Let dry overnight, then apply 2 coats of polyurethane, using the Poly-Brush. Allow to dry between coats, sand with 400-grit sandpaper, and wipe with the tack cloth as required.

**Note:** You can strip off the original paint or varnish, using Dad's Easy Spray Paint, Stain & Varnish Remover, or sand and prime following the directions, above.

# Cabinet Secrets

## Cover up an old cabinet

### WHAT TO DO

**1.** Lay out the drop cloth and set the cabinet on it. Remove all handles and hardware. Sand the cabinet inside and out and wipe clean with the tack cloth. Apply 1 coat of primer/sealer, using the Whizz roller. Let dry, lightly sand and wipe clean with the tack cloth.

**2.** Using the Poly-Brush, paint entire surface with *Raw Umber* Crackle Base Coat paint. Let dry overnight.

**3.** Dampen a small piece of the sea sponge with water. Pour some *Tan* Crackle Top Coat paint into a saucer. Dip the sponge in it, then dab all over the cabinet. Let dry overnight.

**4.** Using a pencil, lightly draw a curving vine pattern over the front and sides.

**5.** Using the ¼-inch brush dipped in a variety of colored blocking glazes, apply a moderate amount of glaze to different leaf printing pads and Americana *Deep Burgundy* paint to the berry-pattern pad, pressing into the cabinet along the pencil line. Reuse the same pad several times without re-applying paint to obtain different effects.

**6.** To paint the vines, pour a little *Clear*, *Brown* and *Teal Green* glazes into a dish. Dip the veining brush in all 3 without mixing the colors together and apply to the cabinet, connecting some of the leaves to the main vine stem. Let dry overnight.

**7.** Spray with 2 coats of acrylic enamel, allowing to dry between coats.

### WHAT YOU NEED

- a wooden cabinet
- Dynamic Plastic Drop Cloth (Heavy Weight)
- 180-grit sandpaper
- Dynamic Tack Cloth
- 1 1-qt/946-mL can Zinsser Cover Stain Primer/Sealer
- Whizz 4-inch Premium Fabric Roller and Tray Set
- 3-inch Poly-Brush
- 2 6-oz/177-mL bottles Symphony Aged/Crackled Finishes – Base Coat Paint, *Raw Umber*
- Dynamic Sea Sponge
- 2 6-oz/177-mL bottles Symphony Aged/Crackled Finishes – Top Coat paint, *Tan*
- pencil
- Dynamic ¼-inch All Purpose Brush
- Cutbill Blocking Glaze: 2 2-oz/59-mL jars each of *Umber Brown*; *Warm Brown*; *Teal Green* 1 2-oz/59-mL jar Blocking Glaze (*clear*)
- 1 2-oz/59-mL bottle DecoArt Americana Acrylic Paint, *Deep Burgundy*
- Cutbill Block Printing Pads: *Generic Leaf* (large) *Generic Leaf* (small) *Berry* (large and small)
- Symphony Veining Brush (*Sable Dagger #10*)
- 1 340-g can Dynamic Water-Based Acrylic Enamel Spray, *Clear*

# *F*rame-ups

*Transform plain frames into works of art*

## Marble magic

### WHAT TO DO

1. Sand the frame. Wipe with the tack cloth to remove dust.

2. Spray with *Black Onyx* base coat, according to the manufacturer's instructions. Let dry.

3. Spray with *White Marble* top coat, according to the manufacturer's instructions. Let dry.

### WHAT YOU NEED

- wood frame
- 180-grit sandpaper
- Dynamic Tack Cloth
- 1 340-g can Crown Marble Ultra Rich Base Coat, *Black Onyx*
- 1 150-g can Crown Marble Decorator Top Coat, *White Marble*

## WHAT YOU NEED

- flat wood frame
- polyester quilt batting
- 40 mL bottle Elmer's Glue-All
- cotton fabric
- piece of chalk
- scissors
- Buckingham Stencil, *Sailpast* (border portion only)
- Buckingham Stencil, *Romanesque Border*
- 1 1-oz/29.6-mL jar DecoArt Easy Blend Stencil Paint, *Glorious Gold*
- 1 1-oz/29.6-mL jar DecoArt Easy Blend Stencil Paint, *Dioxazine Purple*
- Buckingham ½-inch Stencil Brush
- staple gun and staples
- piece of mirror
- decorative beads (optional)

# Stencil it!

## WHAT TO DO

1. Cut out the quilt batting so that it is slightly larger than the frame. Cut out the *hole* in the middle. Apply small dots of glue randomly over the front of the frame. Press batting on top.

2. Lay the fabric right-side up on a flat surface. Make sure there is sufficient fabric to cover the front and back of the frame. Center the frame on it. Using chalk, trace an outline of the frame, including the *hole* cutout, onto the fabric. Remove the frame.

3. Using stencils and paints as pictured, create a pattern on the right side of the fabric. Let the paint dry thoroughly.

4. Cut out the fabric, allowing enough to wrap around the frame to the back side. Miter the corner edges. Lay the fabric wrong-side up on a flat surface; lay the padded frame wrong-side up on top. Pull the fabric around to the underside of the frame and staple in place. Set the mirror in the frame. Glue or use small nails to hold it in place.

5. Cut another piece of fabric exactly the size as the frame. Glue it to the back of the frame. Sew decorative beads to the padded front, if desired.

# Border Lines

*Stencil a parade of dinosaurs around a playroom*

## WHAT TO DO

**1.** Wearing gloves, clean the area to be painted with a rag moistened with paint thinner. Wipe dry with another clean rag. (Let cloth dry completely before throwing it out.) Sand the surface, if necessary, and wipe with the tack cloth.

**2.** Press painter's tape firmly on the floor 3 inches away from the baseboard all around the room. Press another line of painter's tape firmly on the floor 11 inches in from the first tape to create an 11-inch wide border.

**3.** Using the roller, apply 1 coat of primer/sealer to the border area between the lines.

**4.** Spray the underside of the stencil with adhesive and press to the floor. Using the stencil brush, paint the designs in the following colors: *Primary Blue* for the large dinosaurs, *Primary Red* and *Primary Yellow* for the smaller dinosaurs, *Kelly Green* and *Sable Brown* for the trees. Carefully remove the stencil and reposition as required until the border is completed around the room.

**5.** Use the small craft brush to add highlights and shading with *Titanium (Snow) White* and *Soft Black*. Let dry overnight.

**6.** Use the Poly-Brush to apply 2 top coats of polyurethane, allow to dry between coats, and sand lightly between coats with 400-grit sandpaper. Let dry, then remove the tapes.

## WHAT YOU NEED

- 1 pair Dynamic Painting and Stripping Gloves
- 1 1-liter can Dynamic Paint Thinner
- clean rags
- 180-grit sandpaper
- Dynamic Tack Cloth
- 1 roll ¾-inch KleenEdge High-Tack Painter's Tape
- 1 1-qt/946-mL can Zinsser Bulls Eye 1-2-3 Primer/Sealer
- Whizz Premium Fabric Roller and Tray Set
- Buckingham Stencil, *Dinosaur Border*
- Buckingham Stencil Adhesive Spray
- DecoArt Americana Acrylic Paint (quantities depend on size of the room) 1 2-oz/59-mL bottle each of: *Primary Blue; Primary Red; Primary Yellow; Kelly Green; Sable Brown; Titanium (Snow) White; Soft Black*
- Buckingham ½-inch Stencil Brush
- Dynamic Craft Brush
- 3-inch Poly-Brush
- 1 1-qt/946-mL can Old Masters H$_2$O Acrylic Polyurethane Interior Finish (satin)
- 400-grit sandpaper

**Note:** This treatment works only on laminate, painted wood or bare wood (i.e., nonvarnished or nonwaxed) flooring and is best in low-traffic areas.

17

## WHAT YOU NEED

- 2 pieces ¾-inch medium density fiberboard (MDF), each 16 inches x 60 inches
- 1 piece ¾-inch MDF, 16 inches x 66 inches
- 180-grit sandpaper
- Dynamic Tack Cloth
- Dynamic 2-inch Ovation Brush
- 1 1-quart/946-mL can Zinsser Bulls Eye 1-2-3 Primer/Sealer
- metal straight edge
- pencil
- 1-inch KleenEdge High-Tack Painter's Tape
- Dynamic Craft Brush
- 4 2-oz/59-mL bottles DecoArt Americana Acrylic Paint, *Titanium (Snow) White*
- 2 2-oz/59-mL bottles DecoArt Americana Acrylic Paint, *Calico Red*
- 1 1-quart/946-mL can Old Masters H₂O Acrylic Polyurethane Interior Finish (*satin*)
- Dynamic 1-inch All Purpose Brush
- 1 1-quart/946-mL can Dynamic *Black* Chalkboard Paint
- 2-inch Poly-Brush
- 2 6-foot/2-m piano hinges and screws
- 6 wood turnings or finials
- 40 mL bottle Elmer's Glue-All

# A Clean Slate

## *Decorate a room with a blackboard divider screen*

### WHAT TO DO

1. Have the lumberyard cut the MDF to size. Sand thoroughly on both sides and along all edges. Wipe clean with the tack cloth. Using the 2-inch brush and primer/sealer, apply 3 coats to the sides and edges of each board, allowing to dry between coats. Sand as required for a smooth surface, wiping with the tack cloth after sanding.

2. On 1 side of each board, draw a light pencil line 3 inches in from each side and down from the top and 5 inches up from the bottom. Using the 1-inch brush, paint this *frame* with 3 coats of *Titanium (Snow) White* paint, allowing to dry between coats and sanding, if necessary, to provide a smooth finish.

3. Using a metal straight edge and a sharp pencil, draw 1-inch squares on a panel, as shown in the picture. The top and side edges have 3 rows of squares; the bottom edge has 5 rows.

4. Press strips of painter's tape along alternate rows of squares, both lengthwise and crosswise. Paint the spaces left showing with *Calico Red*, using the small craft brush. Let the paint dry, then repeat 2 more times until a deep-red color results. Let dry, then remove the tapes.

5. Press strips of painter's tape across the rows in both directions where you have already painted. Paint with 3 coats of *Calico Red* in the squares left exposed, thus creating the checkerboard pattern. Allow to dry between coats. When the paint is dry, remove the tapes. Repeat these steps on all 3 panels. Let dry thoroughly.

6. Using the 1-inch brush, apply 2 coats of polyurethane to the checkerboard areas only, allowing to dry between coats.

7. Press strips of painter's tape firmly along the first inside rows of checkerboard to create a smooth edge for painting with the chalkboard paint. Using the 2-inch Poly-Brush, apply the chalkboard paint evenly. Let dry thoroughly, and repeat as necessary to obtain desired finish. Let dry, then remove the tapes.

8. Cut the piano hinges to fit exactly. Screw them to the side edges of the panels so that 1 end panel opens to the front and 1 opens to the back.

9. Paint the wood turnings with several coats of red paint, followed by 2 coats of polyurethane, allowing to dry between coats. Glue to the top corners of each panel.

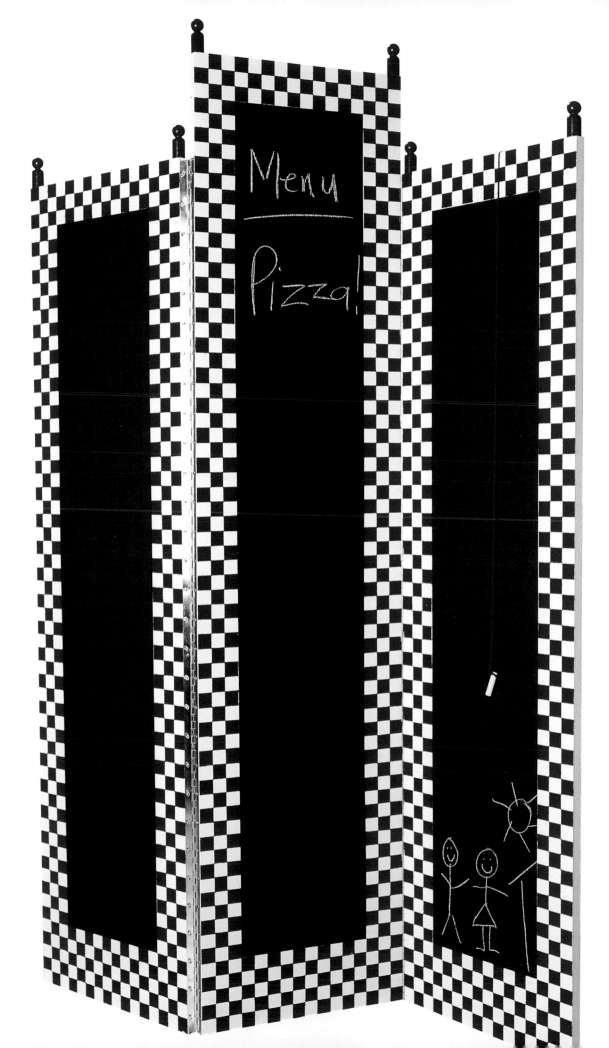

# Fit To Be Tiled

*Stamp ceramic tiles with pleasing motifs*

## WHAT YOU NEED

- ceramic tiles
- 1 1-qt/946-mL can Flood ESP Easy Surface Prep
- clean rags
- DecoArt Ultra Gloss Air Dry Enamel Paint: 1 1-oz/29.6-mL bottle each of: *Christmas Red*; *Lemon Yellow*; *Christmas Green*; *Orange*
- Buckingham Stencil Roller and Tray
- Cutbill Block Printing Pads in the following shapes: *apple*, *pear*, *peach*
- Dynamic Craft Brush

## WHAT TO DO

1. Clean the tiles with ESP and a rag, following the manufacturer's instructions. Wipe dry with a clean rag.

2. Pour about ¼ cup of the desired color of paint into the stencil roller tray, run the roller through the paint and then onto the printing pads. Do not overload the pads with paint.

3. Press the stamps onto the tiles. If you are not pleased with the look, wipe off the paint with a damp cloth and repeat.

4. Paint leaves and stems with the craft brush. Let dry for 7 days before washing or wiping, to be certain the paint is permanent.

**Note:** For this project to work, you must use the exact product specified.

# Clever Headboard

*Create a trompe l'oeil headboard using a projection stencil*

### WHAT TO DO

1. Lay the drop cloth on the floor in front of the wall where the headboard will be created.

2. Follow the directions in the Projection Stenciling Kit to create a headboard to fit the bed. To re-create the colors used, mix 4 parts *Black* and 1 part *Pewter* paint.

### WHAT YOU NEED

- Dynamic Plastic Drop Cloth (Heavy Weight)
- Projection Stenciling Kit, *Wrought Iron Bed* (stencil and directions are included)
- overhead projector
- 1 box 15 m-x-45 cm freezer paper
- Buckingham Stencil Spray Adhesive
- Dynamic All Metal Junior Snap-Off Cutter
- 1 8-oz/225-mL bottle Buckingham Roller Stencil Paint, *Black*
- 1 2-oz/59-mL bottle DecoArt Dazzling Metallics Paint, *Pewter*
- 1 roll ¾-inch KleenEdge High-Tack Painter's Tape

## WHAT YOU NEED

- 1 1-qt/946-mL can Flood ESP Easy Surface Prep
- 1 1-qt/946-mL can Zinsser B-I-N Primer/Sealer
- 2 2-inch Whizz Foam Roller and Handle Sets
- Buckingham Stencil Roller
- DecoArt Ultra Gloss Air Dry Enamel Paint:
  4 1-oz/29.6-mL bottles *Buttermilk*
  1 1-oz/29.6-mL bottle each of *Sable Brown*; *Lemon Yellow*; *Gloss Black*
- 3-inch Poly-Brush
- Buckingham Stencil Roller Refill
- Dynamic Tack Cloth
- 1 1-qt/946-mL can latex paint tinted to match Ultra Gloss Air Dry Enamel, *Sable Brown*
- Dynamic Sea Sponge, about 1 inch in diameter
- 1 1-qt/946-mL can Old Masters $H_2O$ Acrylic Polyurethane Interior Finish (*satin*)
- 400-grit sandpaper
- 1 roll ¾-inch KleenEdge High-Tack Painter's Tape
- vinegar
- Buckingham Stencil Spray Adhesive
- Buckingham Stencil, *Leopard Skin Border*
- Buckingham ½-inch Stencil Brush
- Dynamic 9 ½-inch Lint Free roller with 10-mm pile
- Dynamic 2-L Plastic Paint Tray and 2 liners

# Animal Instincts

*Pep up a powder room with stenciled glamour*

## WHAT TO DO

### For the counter:

1. Remove all hardware from drawers and doors. Clean the countertop and cupboard with ESP, according to the manufacturer's instructions.

2. Using the Whizz roller, apply 1-2-3 Primer/Sealer to the countertop and doors. Let dry for 1 hour.

3. Using the Buckingham Stencil Roller, apply 1 coat of *Buttermilk* Ultra Gloss to the countertop. Let dry. While this is drying, paint the cupboard doors with the Whizz roller and latex paint tinted to match *Sable Brown*. Let dry, lightly sand, wipe clean with the tack cloth and apply a second coat.

4. Pour a little *Sable Brown* UltraGloss paint into a dish. Dip the sea sponge into it and lightly dab paint over the counter in a random pattern, covering about 50 percent of the surface. Wash out the sponge.

5. Pour a little *Lemon Yellow* paint into a dish. Dip the sponge in the paint and dab on the counter, covering about 25 percent of the surface and overlapping the first color in places. Wash out the sponge.

6. Pour a little *Gloss Black* paint into a dish. Dip the sponge in the paint and lightly dab on the counter, covering about 10 percent of the surface. Let dry.

7. Using the Poly-Brush, apply polyurethane to the countertop and doors. Let dry, sand lightly, wipe with the tack cloth and apply a second coat.

- 1 1-gal/3.8-L can latex paint (eggshell finish), tinted to match *Buttermilk* UltraGloss paint
- Dynamic Drop Cloth
- Dynamic 2-inch Ovation Brush
- 2 Dynamic cage frames
- 1 22-oz/650-mL bottle Zinsser Blend & Glaze Extender (latex)
- 1 1-qt/946-mL can Zinsser Blend & Glaze Decorative Painting Liquid (latex)
- small pail or clean empty 1-gallon can
- Ritins Studio Series Floppy Roller – Large
- 1-inch Poly-Brush

BEFORE

**For the mirror:**

1. Press tape around the mirror, 4 ½ inches/11.5 cm in from the edge. Wipe the border area with a cloth or paper towel moistened with vinegar. Dry thoroughly.

2. Using the Buckingham Stencil Roller, apply 1 coat of UltraGloss *Buttermilk* paint to the border. Let dry. Apply a second coat lightly.

3. Repeat steps No. 4 and 5 for the counter. Let dry.

4. Spray the underside of the stencil and press onto the mirror frame. Pour some *Gloss Black* paint into the roller tray; roll the roller in the paint and up the sloped edge until most of the paint has been left behind and the roller feels almost *dry*. Roll the roller over the stencil, creating black spots. Carefully remove the stencil, re-apply it and paint until the frame is completely spotted. For hard-to-reach areas, use the stencil brush to apply the black paint. Do not varnish the mirror frame. Let dry overnight, then carefully remove the tape.

**For the walls:**

1. Spread out drop cloth and protect anything you don't want to paint, with tape.

2. Insert a tray liner into the paint tray and pour in latex paint color-matched to *Buttermilk* Ultra Gloss paint. Use the Ovation brush and the 10 mm-pile roller to paint the walls. Let dry, sand and apply a second coat. Let dry.

3. Mix the glaze in the pail: combine half the *Sable Brown*-colored latex paint with 1 bottle Blend & Glaze Extender and 1 can Decorative Painting Liquid. Stir well.

4. Pour the glaze into a paint tray fitted with a fresh liner and roll it onto the wall. Cover about 4 feet square at a time. Paint the glaze into the corners with the Ovation brush and then roll glaze onto the wall. Wet the Floppy Roller and wring it out so that it is barely damp. Fit it onto the second cage frame. Roll it over the fresh glaze while it is still wet until the desired look is achieved. Work fast! Once you have started a wall, do not stop until wall is complete

**Note:** This treatment is recommended for a powder room that is not heavily used.

# Spot On!

*Stencil a leopard-spot mirror frame*

## WHAT YOU NEED

- flat wood frame, either new or used
- 180-grit sandpaper
- Dynamic Tack Cloth
- Dynamic 1-inch All Purpose Brush
- DecoArt Americana Acrylic Paint:
  1 2-oz/59-mL bottle each of *Desert Sand*; *Toffee*; *Khaki Tan*; *Lamp (Ebony) Black*
- 1 2-oz/59-mL bottle Dazzling Metallics Acrylic Paint, *Emperor's Gold*
- Dynamic Sea Sponge, approximately 2 inches in diameter
- Buckingham Stencil, *Leopard Skin Border*
- Buckingham Stencil Adhesive Spray
- Buckingham ½-inch Stencil Brush
- Dynamic Craft Brush
- 1 1-qt/946-mL can Old Masters $H_2O$ Acrylic Polyurethane Interior Finish (*satin*)
- 400-grit sandpaper
- decorative wooden scroll
- 40 mL bottle Elmer's Glue-All (optional)
- piece of mirror to fit the frame

## WHAT TO DO

1. Sand the frame thoroughly with 180-grit sandpaper until very smooth. Wipe with the tack cloth to remove particles.

2. Using the 1-inch brush, paint the frame with 3 coats of *Desert Sand* paint, sanding between coats. Wipe with the tack cloth.

3. Pour a small amount of *Toffee* paint into a saucer. Dip a small piece of sponge in the paint and dab lightly in a strip along the 2 vertical frame borders and in another strip about 6 inches wide in the center of the top and bottom horizontal frame borders. Rinse out the sponge and squeeze dry. Let the paint dry.

4. Pour a small amount of *Khaki Tan* paint in a saucer. Dip the sponge in the paint and dab lightly on top of the first coat of dabbed-on paint, but make the strips about half an inch narrower in each case. Rinse out the sponge and let the paint dry.

5. Spray the underside of the stencil with adhesive. Position the stencil on the frame. Pour a small amount of *Lamp (Ebony) Black* paint in a saucer. Dip the stencil brush in the paint, dab off excess paint on a piece of paper and then lightly jab at the openings of the stencil. Reposition the stencil as required, taking care not to smudge wet paint on the frame. Let the paint dry.

6. Using the small craft brush, paint the outside edge of the frame with *Lamp (Ebony) Black* paint. Let dry and repeat with a second coat. Likewise, paint the inside edge of the frame with 2 or 3 coats of *Emperors Gold* paint.

7. When the paint is dry, use the 1-inch brush to apply two or three coats of polyurethane, allowing to dry between coats and lightly sanding with 400-grit sandpaper to remove any small bumps that may appear in the polyurethane. (The surface will be slightly *textured* where the leopard pattern appears.)

8. Paint the reverse side of the frame, using the 1-inch brush and *Lamp (Ebony) Black* paint. Two coats may be necessary. Then, apply 2 coats of polyurethane, allowing to dry between coats.

9. If desired, paint a decorative scroll with 3 coats of *Emperor's Gold* paint, allowing to dry between coats. Apply polyurethane, let dry. Then, glue to the top of the frame.

10. Insert the mirror in the frame.

# Faux-Finished Fantasy

## Faux-marble bathroom cabinets for a fantastic look

### WHAT TO DO

**1.** Lightly sand the areas to be painted with 180-grit sandpaper and wipe clean with the tack cloth. Apply ESP, following the manufacturer's instructions. Wipe clean.

**2.** Apply 1 coat of primer/sealer, using the 3-inch brush. Let dry. Apply 2 coats of latex paint, allowing to dry and sanding between coats with 180-grit sandpaper.

**3.** Follow the directions on the Symphony Portofino Marble Kit. When dry, apply 2 coats of polyurethane using the Poly-Brush, sanding between coats with 400-grit sandpaper.

**BEFORE**

### WHAT YOU NEED

- 180-grit sandpaper
- Dynamic Tack Cloth
- 1 1-qt/946-mL can Flood ESP Easy Surface Prep
- cloths
- 1 1-qt/946-mL can ZinsserBulls Eye 1-2-3 Primer/Sealer
- 3-inch Poly-Brush
- Symphony Portofino Marble Kit
- 1 1-pt/473-mL can latex paint, *ivory-colored*\*
- Dynamic 2-inch Ovation Brush
- Decorative Glazes: 1 6-oz/177-mL bottle each of *Golden Yellow; Mocha; Black Onyx*
- 1 1-qt/946-mL can Old Masters $H_2O$ Acrylic Polyurethane Interior Finish (*satin*)
- 400-grit sandpaper

\* In this bathroom the fixtures were ivory, so the background color of the marble is ivory, instead of white, as recommended in the kit. Adjust your background colors to suit your room.

## WHAT YOU NEED

- peel-and-stick lampshade
- natural-colored cotton fabric (for a 10-inch shade, ⅔ yd fabric is required)
- DecoArt Americana Acrylic Paint:
  1 2-oz/59-mL bottle each of *Desert Sand; Toffee; Khaki Tan; Lamp (Ebony) Black*
  1 2-oz/59-mL bottle textile medium
- Dynamic Sea Sponge, approximately 1 inch in diameter
- Buckingham Stencil, *Leopard Skin Border*
- Buckingham ¼-inch Stencil Brush
- iron
- 40 mL Bottle Elmer's Glue-All
- hot glue gun and glue sticks
- 1½ yds decorative upholstery trim

# Shady Deal

*Use fabric paint and a stencil to customize a lampshade*

## WHAT TO DO

1. Remove the paper covering from the peel-and-stick lampshade and trace around it onto the right side of the fabric.

2. Pour about ½ tablespoon of *Desert Sand* paint into a saucer and add ¼ tablespoon of textile medium to it. Stir together well. Dip the sponge into the paint and lightly dab it all over the fabric within the lines that mark off the shade. Repeat the process, using *Toffee* and *Khaki Tan* paint mixed with textile medium. Let dry.

3. Mix about 2 tablespoons of *Lamp (Ebony) Black* paint in a saucer with 1 tablespoon textile medium. Position the stencil on the fabric. Using the stencil brush, dab the paint in the openings. Carefully reposition the stencil until the shade is totally painted with spots.

4. Let dry overnight. Cover the fabric with a pressing cloth. With the iron set on *hot*, press for 30 seconds. Cut out the shade. Fold ¼ inch of fabric to the underside along one vertical end edge, to make a smooth seam at the back of the shade.

5. Following the directions on the shade, position the fabric in place. Press firmly, smoothing the fabric so that no bubbles appear. Use Elmer's Glue-All to close the seam.

6. Use hot glue to attach trim to the top and bottom edges of the shade, joining the ends at the seam line.

# Stripe It Rich

*Create a stunning dresser from an everyday chest of drawers*

**BEFORE**

## WHAT YOU NEED

- Dynamic Plastic Drop Cloth (Heavy Weight)
- painted or varnished wooden dresser
- Dynamic Painting and Stripping Gloves
- 1 1-qt/946-mL can Dad's Easy Spray Paint, Stain & Varnish Remover
- Dynamic 3-inch Putty Knife
- Dynamic Brass Mini Wire Scratch Brush
- Rhodes Steel Wool, #2
- 1 1-L can Dynamic Paint Thinner
- Dynamic Cheese Cloth
- 180-grit sandpaper
- Dynamic Tack Cloth
- 2-inch KleenEdge High-Tack Painter's Tape
- Old Masters Thick 'n EZY Gel Stain:
  1 ½-pt/236-mL can *Pickling White*
  1 ½-pt/236-mL can *Cherry*
- 1 1-qt/946-mL can Old Masters Poly Plastic Polyurethane (*satin*)
- 3-inch Poly-Brush
- 1 2-oz/59-mL jar Cutbill Latex Block Printing Glaze, *Copper Metallic* (optional)
- Dynamic Craft Brush (optional)

## WHAT TO DO

**1.** Spread out the drop cloth in the work area, which should be well ventilated or outdoors. Wearing gloves, spray a generous even layer of remover on the dresser. Let stand for 20 minutes.

**2.** Use the putty knife to scrape off the blistered finish. Use the scratch brush for hard-to-reach areas. Spray again and let stand for 10 minutes, then rub down with steel wool dipped in paint thinner. Wipe clean with cheese cloth. If necessary, sand, then wipe clean with the tack cloth.

3. Press strips of tape side-by-side over the entire dresser. Remove alternate tapes.

4. Stir *Pickling White* gel stain. Using cheese cloth, apply 2 or 3 coats, allowing to dry, sand between coats, then wipe with the tack cloth. Let dry.

5. Remove the tapes, then press fresh tapes over the stained strips. Using a soft cloth, apply 2 coats of *Cherry* stain, following the directions, above.

6. Apply 2 coats of polyurethane, using the Poly-Brush, allowing to dry between coats. Sand as required and wipe with the tack cloth.

7. Optional: accent with *Copper* stripes for added effect. Use the craft brush to paint a thin line of *Copper Metallic* glaze where the stripes meet.

STEP 2

STEP 4

## WHAT YOU NEED

- metal filing cabinet
- Dynamic Drop Cloth
- Dynamic All Purpose Disposable Latex Gloves
- Dynamic Cheese Cloth
- 1 1-liter can Dynamic Paint Thinner
- 180-grit sandpaper
- Dynamic Tack Cloth
- Whizz 4-inch Premium Fabric Roller and Tray Set
- 1 1-pt-/473-mL can Zinsser B-I-N Primer/Sealer
- 2 3-inch Poly-Brushes
- 1 1-qt/947-mL can Old Masters Graining Base, *Driftwood*
- 1 ½-pt/236-mL can Old Masters THICK 'n EZY Gel Stain in the following colors: *Natural; Golden Oak; Dark Walnut*
- Symphony Triangular Graining Comb
- Symphony Badger Brush
- metal straight edge
- pencil
- 1 roll ¾-inch KleenEdge High-Tack Painter's Tape
- Dynamic 2-inch Ovation Brush
- Dynamic Craft Brush
- 1 1-qt/946-mL can Old Masters Poly Plastic Polyurethane (*satin*)
- 400-grit sandpaper

# Top Drawer!

## *Makeover a metal file cabinet with a wood-grain finish*

### WHAT TO DO

**1.** Set the filing cabinet on the drop cloth. Wearing disposable gloves, wipe the cabinet with cheese cloth dipped in paint thinner. Wipe dry. (Let cloth dry completely before throwing it out.) Sand the cabinet, then wipe clean with the tack cloth. Using the Whizz roller, apply 1 coat of primer/sealer. Let dry approximately 1 hour.

**2.** Using a Poly-Brush, apply 1 coat of *Driftwood* graining base over the entire cabinet. Let dry. Using another Poly-Brush, apply 1 coat of *Golden Oak* stain. While wet, create wood graining by pulling the graining comb across the surface. Soften the marks with the badger brush. Let dry.

**3.** On top of the cabinet, draw an "X" from corner to corner, using the pencil and straight edge. Press tape along the lines so that you can paint the 2 triangles on the *side* of the top. With a Poly-Brush, apply *Natural* stain on these 2 triangles. While wet, lightly brush on some *Dark Walnut* stain. Use the graining comb to create the wood grain; soften the lines with the badger brush. Let dry.

**4.** Repeat step No.3 on the front drawers and side panels.

**5.** To create burled walnut panels on the sides, press on tape in the desired shape. Using a Poly-Brush, apply *Natural* stain inside the taped-off areas. While stain is still wet, lightly apply *Dark Walnut* stain with a Poly-Brush. Using the Ovation brush, brush out the gel to create a random grain pattern. Pull the graining comb over this area, using a jerky motion. Using the craft brush, lightly paint in some darker grain and a few random dark spots. Blend and soften with the badger brush. Let dry.

**6.** Use a Poly-Brush to apply 1 coat of polyurethane. Let dry, then sand lightly with 400-grit sandpaper. Wipe with the tack cloth. Apply a second coat of polyurethane.

## WHAT YOU NEED

- old metal tray
- 180-grit sandpaper
- Dynamic Tack Cloth
- Dynamic 1-inch All Purpose Brush
- 1 2-oz/57-mL jar Dynamic Enamel Paint each of: *Chocolate Brown; Flat Black*
- ¾-inch Kleen Edge High-Tack Painter's Tape
- 1 2-oz/57-mL jar Dynamic Metallic Leaf Finish Paint, *Copper*
- scissors
- 1 1-qt/946-mL can Flood Penetrol
- toothpick
- Dynamic All Purpose Disposable Latex Gloves
- old toothbrush
- Symphony Badger Brush
- 1 1-liter can Dynamic Paint Thinner
- 1 340-g can Dynamic Enamel Spray Paint - Urethane Gloss *Clear*
- Rhodes Steel Wool, #0000

# Carried Away

*Treat cast-off trays to makeovers*

## Shimmering server

## WHAT TO DO

1. Lightly sand the tray and wipe with the tack cloth to remove all particles. Using the 1-inch brush, apply 1 coat of *Chocolate Brown* paint. Let dry. Apply a second coat, if necessary. Let dry.

2. Cut strips of tape in half lengthwise and press them on the tray in wavy criss-cross patterns.

3. Using the 1-inch brush, paint the exposed surface with *Copper* Metallic Leaf Finish Paint. Let dry. Remove the tapes.

4. Mix a little *Flat Black* paint with an equal amount of Penetrol, stirring with the toothpick. Wearing gloves, dip the toothbrush in the mixture and flick it onto the tray. Brush it out with the badger brush. Dry off the toothbrush, then dip it into paint thinner and flick over the tray. Brush out with the badger brush. Let dry.

5. Spray with at least 2 coats of enamel urethane spray. Allow to dry and sand with steel wool between coats.

# Tray chic

## WHAT TO DO

1. Lightly sand the tray in the direction of the wood grain. Wipe clean with the tack cloth.

2. Using the Poly-Brush, apply 1 coat of *Natural* stain. Let dry overnight.

3. Enlarge the fish stencil on a photocopier until it is approximately 10 inches long or until it suits the size of your tray and allows for borders, as shown in the photograph.

4. Trace the tray onto the shiny side of a piece of freezer paper. Draw a circle 1 inch from the edge and another circle ¼ inch inside that. Trace around the fish stencil, centering it in the middle of the circles. Spray the underside of the paper with adhesive spray and press firmly in place on the tray.

5. Using the snap-off cutter, trace around the pencil marks, scoring through the paper and into the wood. (This will provide the illusion of *inlaid* wood.)

6. Peel off the sections of paper as you stain certain areas. After the stain has dried, replace the paper to protect some areas while staining others. Peel away the paper covering the fish. Pour a little *Dark Mahogany* stain onto a piece of paper; dab the stencil brush in it, then dab off the excess on another piece of paper until the brush is almost dry. Dab the brush over the exposed wood. Let dry.

7. Repeat the stenciling for the remaining areas as follows: stain the outer ring with *Dark Walnut*, then stain the inner ring with *Cherry*. Let dry overnight.

8. Spray with 2 coats of polyurethane, allowing to dry between coats.

## WHAT YOU NEED

- large round wooden serving tray or platter
- 400-grit sandpaper
- Dynamic Tack Cloth
- 1-inch Poly-Brush
- 1 ½-pt/236-mL cans each of Old Masters THICK 'n EZY Gel Stain: *Natural; Dark Mahogany; Dark Walnut; Cherry*
- Buckingham Stencil, *Salmon*
- freezer paper
- Buckingham Stencil Adhesive Spray
- Dynamic All Metal Junior Snap-Off Cutter
- Buckingham ½-inch Stencil Brush
- 1 13-oz/368-g can Old Masters Poly Plastic Polyurethane Spray *(semi-gloss)*

## WHAT YOU NEED

- Decorplate clear plastic switch or plug plate
- decorative paper or wallcovering
- metal straight edge
- Dynamic All Metal Junior Snap-Off Cutter

# Switched On

*Make electrical coverplates match the decor*

## WHAT TO DO

1. Using the back plate as a template, lay it on the underside of the paper. (If using wallcovering to match walls, be sure the pattern matches the wall exactly.) Trace around with a pencil. Then, use a metal straight edge and Snap-Off Cutter to cut out the paper.

2. Carefully cut out holes for switches or plugs.

3. Sandwich the paper between the two pieces and snap in place. Screw to the wall.

# Bovine Beauty

*Cover a tabletop with faux cowhide*

## WHAT TO DO

**1.** Lightly sand the table. Wipe with the tack cloth to remove all dust. Spray the legs and sides of the table with primer/sealer. Let dry.

**2.** Using the ½-inch brush, apply a thick coat of *White* base coat. Let dry.

**3.** Use the same brush to apply a coat of *Black* top coat. The paint will crack as it dries.

**4.** Spray the legs with *Gloss Clear* enamel spray.

**5.** Using a pencil, trace the tabletop shape on the underside of the Tye-Tac. Cut out with scissors. Remove the backing paper and press the vinyl onto the tabletop.

## WHAT YOU NEED

- small table
- 180-grit sandpaper
- Dynamic Tack Cloth
- 1 13-oz/384-mL spray can Zinsser Cover Stain Primer/Sealer
- Dynamic ½-inch All Purpose Brush
- 1 6-oz/177-mL jar Symphony Aged/Crackled Finishes Base Coat, *White*
- 1 6-oz/177-mL jar Symphony Aged/Crackled Finishes Top Coat, *Black*
- 1 12-oz/340-g can Dynamic Water-Based Acrylic Enamel Spray, *Gloss Clear*
- 1 roll Tye-Tac decorative vinyl, *Cow Spots*
- scissors

# Exciting exterior projects

Take a close look at the furniture and accessories in your garden or on your patio, deck or balcony. Are they showing signs of having spent one too many summers (or winters) outdoors without any maintenance? Do they look as if they are waiting for a makeover? Take another look: do your outdoor furnishings and decorative accents strike you as dull and boring? Would paint add some pizzazz to the patio?

Perhaps you have seen some tempting outdoor accents in hardware stores and garden centers. Maybe they strike you as mass-made and impersonal. If only ..., you think, imagining some colorful way of putting your personal stamp on a few basic items. Chairs, arbors, flowerpots and birdbaths all can easily be trans-formed into unique garden accessories using new easy-to-apply products.

Read on: this chapter brims with great ideas for the outdoors. Some projects are so easy, even the most inexperienced person can attempt them with no fear of failure, while other projects require some previous experience and patience.

## WHAT YOU NEED

- picnic table
- 1 1-quart/946-mL can Flood Dekswood Cleaner and Brightener for Exterior Wood
- Dynamic 3-inch Stain Brush
- 1 1-gal/3.78-L can Flood Solid Color Deck & Siding Stain, *Chamois*
- 180-grit sandpaper
- ¾-inch KleenEdge High-Tack Painter's Tape
- Buckingham Stencil Paint Roller
- DecoArt Patio Paint: 1 8-oz/236-mL bottle each of *Cloud White*; *Summer Sky Blue* 1 2-oz/59-mL bottle each of *Fern Green*; *Sunshine Yellow*
- Buckingham Stencil, *Gingham*
- Buckingham Stencil Adhesive Spray
- Paint Design Stamp, *Daisy*, and Velcro mounting pad
- Dynamic Craft Brush

# Perky Picnic Table

*Make dining out a special occasion with a daisy stamp and gingham stencil*

## WHAT TO DO

**1.** Clean the picnic table, seats and legs with Dekswood, following the manufacturer's instructions. Let dry. Using the stain brush, paint the wood with 2 coats of deck stain, allowing to dry and sanding lightly between coats.

### For the placemats:

**1.** Firmly press painter's tape on the tabletop to create 10-x-18-inch areas for painting 4 (or more) placemats. Using the stencil paint roller and *Cloud White* paint, paint inside the lines. Let dry, then apply a second coat. Let dry. Remove the tapes.

**2.** Spray the underside of the *Gingham* stencil with adhesive and place over the background color of the placemat. Pour some *Summer Sky Blue* paint into a saucer. Using the stencil paint roller, apply color to the stencil, covering the area with vertical lines. Let the paint dry, then rotate the stencil 90 degrees and stencil in lines in the opposite direction, using the same paint. Let dry.

**3.** To create a fringe (optional), use a craft brush to make short fine lines with the same paint colors.

**For the seats:**

**1.** Attach the rubber flower shape of the *Daisy* stamp to the Velcro mounting pad. Pour *Cloud White* paint into the roller tray and roll the roller in it to distribute the paint evenly. Pass the roller over the stamp design; press the stamp onto the seat. Repeat until you have stamped flowers on the the seats where desired. Let dry.

**2.** Remove *daisy* stamp and attach the *stem-and-leaf* stamp to the mounting pad. Pour *Fern Green* paint into the tray and apply it to the stamp in the same way as for the flowers. Press in place at the bottom of each daisy.

**3.** Paint the center of each flower, using the craft brush dipped in *Sunshine Yellow* paint.

## Bug Off!

*Perch sprightly ladybugs all over an arbor*

### WHAT YOU NEED

- a wooden arbor
- 1 1-quart/946-mL can Flood Dekswood Cleaner and Brightener for Exterior Wood
- 1 1-gal/3.78-L can Flood Solid Color Deck & Siding Stain, *Chamois*
- Dynamic 2-inch Ovation Brush
- Dynamic Just 4 Kidz Stencil, *Bugs*
- Buckingham Stencil Adhesive Spray
- DecoArt Patio Paint: 1 2-oz/59-mL bottle each of *Geranium Red*; *Wrought Iron Black*
- Buckingham ½-inch Stencil Brush

**BEFORE**

### WHAT TO DO

**1.** Clean the arbor with Dekswood, following the manufacturer's instructions. Let dry. Using the 2-inch brush, apply 2 coats of *Chamois* deck stain, allowing to dry between coats.

**2.** Spray the underside of the ladybug-body stencil with adhesive. Make marks on the arbor where ladybugs are to be painted. Pour a little *Geranium Red* paint into a saucer. Dip the stencil brush in the paint, then dab off the excess on a piece of paper. Apply the paint to the stencil cut-outs in a swirling motion. Carefully remove the stencil and reposition it. Continue until you have applied as many ladybugs as desired. Let dry.

**3.** Position the spots-and-head stencil on the lady bugs and paint, using *Wrought Iron Black* paint and the stencil brush.

## WHAT YOU NEED

- Dynamic Just 4 Kidz Stencil, *Bugs*

- 1 sheet Buckingham Clear Mylar, 20 inches x 24 inches

- Dynamic All Metal Junior Snap-Off Cutter

- concrete patio stones, 11½ inches in diameter

- Dynamic 1-inch All Purpose Brush

- DecoArt Patio Paint (enough for 4 patio stones) in the following colors:
  1 8-oz/236-mL bottle *Antique Mum*
  1 2-oz/59-mL bottle each of:
  *Light Waterfall Blue*; *Summer Sky Blue*; *Wrought Iron Black*; *Geranium Red*; *Sunshine Yellow*; *Fern Green*; *Light Eucalyptus Green*; *Foxglove Pink*

- Buckingham Stencil Adhesive Spray

- ¾-inch KleenEdge High-Tack Painter's Tape (optional)

- Buckingham ½-inch Stencil Brush

# Step On It!

### *Stencil patio stones along a garden path*

## WHAT TO DO

1. Enlarge the bug stencils on a photocopier until they are approximately 8 inches in diameter. Trace the shapes onto a piece of Mylar and cut out stencils, using the cutter.

2. Paint the top of each patio stone with 2 coats of *Antique Mum*, using the 1-inch brush, allowing to dry between coats. Paint a border around the edge with 2 coats of *Light Waterfall Blue* paint. Let dry.

3. Spray the underside of the stencil and press onto the stone. (You may also require KleenEdge High-Tack Painter's Tape to hold it in place.) Using the following colors and the ½-inch stencil brush, create an assortment of bugs: for the butterflies, use *Summer Sky Blue*, *Wrought Iron Black* and *Geranium Red*. For the bee, use *Sunshine Yellow* and *Wrought Iron Black*. For the dragonflies, use *Fern Green* and purple (mix equal amounts of *Summer Sky Blue* and *Geranium Red* together), and *Light Eucalyptus Green* and *Foxglove Pink*.

# Hit The Deck

## Customize a deck with a painted carpet

### WHAT TO DO

1. Prepare the deck: clean with Dekswood, according to the manufacturer's instructions. Wait for the amount of time specified on the product label before painting the carpet.

2. Press the painter's tape firmly against the deck floor to create an area 4 feet x 5 feet. Mix 3 parts *Antique Mum* paint with 1 part water. Using the Whizz roller, paint within the lines. Let dry, then apply a second coat of full-strength paint.

3. Press tape inside the first outline to create a 4-inch border on all sides. Using the Whizz roller and tray, apply 2 coats of *Patio Brick* paint within the lines, allowing to dry between coats. Remove the tape when the paint is thoroughly dry.

4. Press tape on top of the *Patio Brick* border, along its inside edge. Press tapes 7 inches inside this border. Using the roller and tray, paint with 2 coats of *Antique Mum* paint, allowing to dry between coats. Remove the tape.

5. Press tapes on top of the inside edge of the *Antique Mum* border and 1 inch inside. Use the roller and tray to apply 2 coats of *Patio Brick* paint, allowing to dry between coats. Remove the tape.

6. Press tape along the inside edge of the narrow *Patio Brick* border. Use the roller and tray to apply 2 coats of *Fern Green* paint, allowing to dry between coats.

7. Spray the underside of the stencil marked "B" with adhesive spray. Place the stencil along the outside edge of the *Antique Mum* border area. Use the stencil brush to paint the stencil with *Fern Green* and *Patio Brick* paint, as shown in the photo. Carefully move the stencil along the border until it is completely filled in.

8. Reverse the stencil, spray the underside and stencil the leaf border along the inside edge of the border, as shown in the photo.

9. Paint fringe as shown, if desired. Mix 1 part Americana Brush 'n Blend Extender with 3 parts *Antique Mum* paint. Dip the badger brush in the paint; pull outward from the edge of the *rug*. Add highlights with the craft brush dipped in *Antique Mum* paint.

**Note:** Cover the painted area with a piece of plywood to protect it during cold winter months.

### WHAT YOU NEED

(FOR A CARPET MEASURING 4 FEET X 5 FEET):

**To prepare the deck (optional):**

- 1 1-qt/946-mL can Flood Dekswood Cleaner and Brightener for Exterior Wood

**To paint the carpet:**

- ¾-inch KleenEdge High-Tack Painter's Tape
- DecoArt Patio Paint: 2 8-oz/236-mL bottles each of: *Antique Mum*; *Patio Brick*; *Fern Green*
- Whizz Premium Fabric Roller and Tray Set (optional: one roller per color)
- Blue Mountain Stencil, *Fantasy Ribbon*
- Blue Mountain Repositionable Stencil Adhesive Spray
- Blue Mountain ½-inch Stencil Brush
- 2-oz/59-mL bottle DecoArt Americana Brush 'n Blend Extender
- Symphony 2-inch Badger Brush (for the fringe)

BEFORE

## WHAT YOU NEED

### For the playhouse:

- a wooden playhouse
- 1 1-gal/3.78-L can Flood Dekswood Cleaner and Brightener for Exterior Wood
- 3 Dynamic plastic paint-tray liners
- 1 3-L Dynamic paint tray
- Flood Solid Color Deck & Siding Stain:
  1 1-gal/3.78-L can each of:
  *Slate Blue*; *Antique Grey*
- 2 Dynamic 9 1/2-inch Poly Pro ½-inch (15-mm) nap rollers
- 1 1-gal/3.78-L can Zinsser Exterior *Perma White* Paint
- Dynamic 9½-inch cage frame
- Whizz 4-inch Premium Roller and Tray Set

### For the gingerbread trim:

- Buckingham Stencil, *Carolina Scroll*
- ¾-inch KleenEdge High-Tack Painter's Tape
- 1 2-oz/59-mL bottle DecoArt Patio Paint, *Cloud White*
- Buckingham Stencil Roller and Tray

### For the window:

- Buckingham Stencil, *Cottage Window*
- ¾-inch KleenEdge High-Tack Painter's Tape
- Buckingham stencil roller and 2-pack refill and tray
- DecoArt Patio Paint:
  1 2-oz/59-mL bottle each of *Concrete Grey*; *Antique Mum*; *Cloud White*
- ½ yd/0.5 m vinyl lace
- Buckingham Stencil Adhesive Spray

# Victorian Fantasy

*Transform a plain playhouse into a cottage charmer*

**BEFORE**

## WHAT TO DO

### For the playhouse:

1. Clean the playhouse with Dekswood, according to the manufacturer's instructions.

2. Insert a tray liner into the paint tray. Stir the *Slate Blue* solid-color stain well and pour some into the paint tray. Using a large roller, apply 2 coats of stain to the front, back and side walls of the house, allowing to dry between coats.

3. Insert a fresh liner in the paint tray. Using the Whizz roller, paint the trim, door, railings and planter boxes with 2 coats of *Perma White* paint, allowing to dry between coats.

4. Insert a fresh tray liner in the paint tray. Stir the *Antique Grey* stain well and pour some into the paint tray. Using a clean large roller, apply 2 coats of stain to the peak, porch floor and inside the playhouse, allowing to dry between coats.

### For the gingerbread trim:

1. Mark the center of the peak. Tape stencil "A" to the left of the mark. Using the stencil roller and tray, apply *Cloud White* paint.

50

Carefully remove the stencil and dry it off. Flip it over and tape to the right of the mark, creating a heart shape in the middle. Stencil as before.

2. Position stencil "B" next to the heart shape and tape in place. Using the stencil roller, apply white paint. Remove the stencil and let the paint dry. Continue stenciling as far as desired.

**For the window:**

1. Tape the window stencil to the door. Trace the outline of the stencil with a pencil. Remove the stencil and press tape outside the pencil lines to form a rectangle.

2. Using *Concrete Grey* Patio Paint and stencil roller, paint inside the tape marks. Let dry.

3. Retape the stencil in position. Using the Buckingham stencil roller and tray, pour *Antique Mum* paint into the tray and roll it onto the *window panes*. Let dry. Remove the stencil.

4. Cut the vinyl lace the same size as the window panes. Spray 1 side of the lace with stencil adhesive and press into place. Using the stencil roller and tray filled with *Cloud White* paint, roll over the lace, forming *curtains*.

5. In the roller stencil tray, mix 1 part *Cloud White* paint with 3 parts *Concrete Grey* to form a lighter grey paint for window shadowing. Tape the next overlay stencil onto the window and roll on the shadow lines, as instructed on the package.

# Metal Urges

*Rescue a rusted dining set in a flash with sprayed-on paint*

## WHAT YOU NEED

- metal patio table (glass top, optional) and chairs
- Dynamic Plastic Drop Cloth
- Dynamic Brass Miniature Wire Scratch Brush
- 3 340-g cans Hammerite Anti-Rust Spray Paint, *White Smooth Finish*
- The Original CAN GUN Aerosol Spray Can Trigger-Handle (optional)
- DecoArt Ultra Gloss Air Dry Enamel Paints and Dynamic Craft Brush (optional)

BEFORE

## WHAT TO DO

1. Remove the existing chair seats and glass top. Set aside. Recover chair seats, if desired.

2. Lay out a drop cloth in the work area. (Do not use newsprint, as the ink may transfer to the painted surface.) Use the wire brush to remove rust and loose paint.

3. Spray a light coat of paint over all surfaces. Let dry, then spray again. You may need to spray several times to cover completely.

4. Replace the chair seats and glass table top. Paint or stencil a design on the glass, using DecoArt Ultra Gloss Air Dry Enamel paints and the craft brush. (Use Cutbill Block Printing Pads, if you prefer. See instructions on page 20: *Fit to Be Tiled.*)

54

# Lighten Up!

*Try a simple solution to brighten outdoor lights*

## WHAT TO DO

**1.** Lay out the drop cloth in your work area, preferably outdoors. If possible, remove the glass from the lamps and set aside. If this is not possible, cover glass areas with tape. Using the wire brush, remove loose rust and paint. If the lamps are new, roughen the surface with the brush to improve paint adhesion.

**2.** Spray with paint. Let dry. Spray again if necessary.

**Note:** For easy cleanup of your hands, apply Gloves in a Bottle skin protectant before starting.

## WHAT YOU NEED

- Dynamic Plastic Drop Cloth
- old rusty lamps or lanterns or new ones
- ¾-inch KleenEdge High-Tack Painter's Tape
- Dynamic Brass Mini Wire Scratch Brush
- 1 340-g can Hammerite Anti-Rust Spray Paint, *Red Hammered Finish*
- 1 340-g can Hammerite Anti-Rust Spray Paint, *Light Blue Hammered Finish*
- 1 bottle Gloves in a Bottle (optional)

# Bath Splash

## Turn a basic birdbath into a special spa with decorative paint

### WHAT TO DO

**1.** Paint the birdbath all over, using the 1-inch brush and *Cloud White* paint. Let dry. Dip the sea sponge in *Antique Mum* paint and dab all over to create a marbled effect.

**2.** Enlarge the pattern for the bowl (page 58) on a photocopier until it fits inside your birdbath. (You may need to tape pieces together to create the correct size.) Place a sheet of carbon paper between your pattern and the bowl and trace the shapes onto the bowl, using a pencil or other pointed object. Use the 1-inch brush to paint the edge with *Deep Waterfall Blue* paint.

**3.** Cut the cellulose sponge into ½-inch, ¾-inch and 1-inch square pieces. Dab the pieces into various paints and then onto the birdbath, to re-create the pattern shown.

**4.** Use the chalk to outline a spiral shape around the column. Dab with sponges dipped in different paints along the spiral line to re-create the pattern shown in the illustration.

### WHAT YOU NEED

- concrete birdbath
- Dynamic 1-inch All Purpose Brush
- Dynamic Sea Sponge, approximately 1 inch in diameter
- 2 sheets black carbon paper
- pencil
- DecoArt Patio Paint:
  1 8-oz/236-mL bottle each of *Cloud White*; *Antique Mum*
  1 2-oz/59-mL bottle each of: *Deep Waterfall Blue*; *Sunflower Yellow*; *Fern Green*; *Patio Brick*; *Light Waterfall Blue*
- Dynamic Cellulose Sponge
- piece of chalk

1 Patio Brick

2 50% Patio Brick 50% Antique Mum

3 Sunflower Yellow

4 50% Sunflower Yellow 50% Antique Mum

5 Cloud White

6 50% Cloud White 50% Light Waterfall Blue

7 Light Waterfall Blue

8 Deep Waterfall Blue

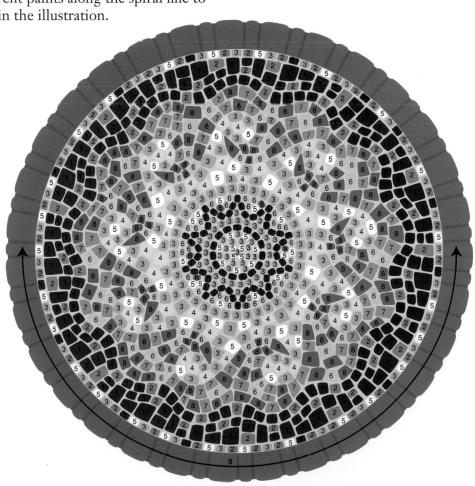

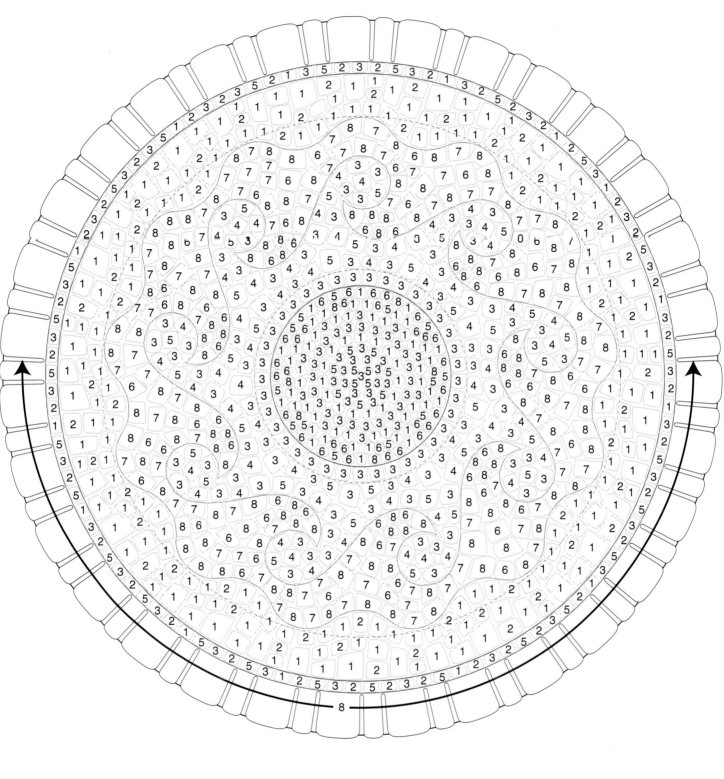

| | 1 | | 2 | | 3 | | 4 | | 5 | | 6 | | 7 | | 8 |

# Birdhouse City

*Give your feathered friends a choice location with three flighty houses*

Any one of our trio of birdhouses gives you an opportunity to decorate big on a small scale. They are so pretty and whimsical, you'll want them indoors as fun accent pieces. (In fact, the first two are weather-friendly, but the glittery one on page 62 is not.)

## Jungle-fever birdhouse

*Stencil a birdhouse with a snazzy pattern*

### WHAT TO DO

**1.** Sand the wood lightly. Wipe clean with the tack cloth.

**2.** Paint all the walls with *Antique Mum* paint, using the 1-inch brush. Let dry, then apply a second coat.

**3.** Using the sea sponge and *Golden Honey* paint, dab a vertical stripe of paint about 2 inches wide on the face of the birdhouse and along each side. Let dry, then repeat using *Pinecone Brown* mixed with a little *Antique Mum* paint, centering the stripe about ½ inch inside the first stripe.

**4.** Spray the underside of the stencil with stencil spray. Press the stencil on the front of the birdhouse. Pour a small amount of *Wrought Iron Black* paint into a saucer. Dab the stencil brush in the paint, then onto a piece of paper to remove excess paint. Then, apply to the openings in the stencil. Apply only enough paint to produce a stippled look. Reposition the stencil as required, taking care not to smudge any wet paint. Use the craft brush to paint spots the stencil cannot reach, such as the peak under the eaves. Repeat for the sides.

**5.** Using the 1-inch brush, paint the roof with *Geranium Red* paint. Let dry, sand lightly and apply a second coat. Let dry.

**6.** Using the 1-inch brush, apply 2 coats of varnish over all surfaces, allowing to dry between coats.

### WHAT YOU NEED

- wooden birdhouse
- 180-grit sandpaper
- Dynamic Tack Cloth
- DecoArt Patio Paint: 1 2-oz/59-mL bottle each of *Antique Mum*; *Golden Honey*; *Pinecone Brown*; *Wrought Iron Black*; *Geranium Red*
- Dynamic 1-inch All Purpose Brush
- Dynamic Sea Sponge, approximately 1 inch in diameter
- Buckingham Stencil, *Leopard Skin Border*
- Buckingham Stencil Adhesive Spray
- Buckingham 1/2-inch Stencil Brush
- Dynamic Craft Brush
- 1 2-oz/59-mL bottle DecoArt DuraClear Exterior/Interior Varnish (*satin*)

# Classical columned birdhouse

## Create a haven for the birds

### WHAT TO DO

1. Using the 1-inch paintbrush, paint the walls and perch with one coat of *Concrete Grey* paint. Let dry.

2. Using the 1-inch paintbrush, paint the walls and perch with several coats of *Natural Beige* Sandstones, allowing to dry between coats.

3. Using the 1-inch paintbrush, paint the roof with 1 coat of *Pot O' Gold* paint. Let dry, then paint with one coat of *Pale Gold* paint. Let dry. Sponge the roof lightly with *Light Eucalyptus Green* paint.

4. Using the fret saw, cut doweling and miniature spools for columns to fit between the platform and eaves. Glue the pieces together as required. When the glue has dried, paint the columns with several coats of Sandstones in the same way as the walls. Glue a piece of textured ribbon to a small thin piece of wood to create the cross-bracing and paint with several coats of Sandstones. Glue the columns and cross-bracing in place.

### WHAT YOU NEED

- wooden birdhouse
- Dynamic 1-inch All Purpose Brush
- 1 2-oz/59-mL bottle DecoArt Patio Paint, *Concrete Grey*
- 2 4-oz/118-mL bottles DecoArt Sandstones, *Natural Beige*
- Dynamic Craft Brush
- 1 2-oz/59-mL bottle DecoArt Patio Paint, *Pot O' Gold*
- 1 2-oz/59-mL bottle DecoArt Royal Metallics, *Pale Gold*
- 1 2-oz/59-mL bottle DecoArt Patio Paint, *Light Eucalyptus Green*
- Dynamic Sea Sponge, approximately 1 inch in diameter
- fret saw
- approx. 8-inch-long piece of ¾-inch-diameter doweling
- miniature spools, ¾ Inch in diameter
- miniature spindles
- 40-mL bottle Elmer's Glue-All
- textured ribbon, approx. ½ inch wide and 6 inches long
- small piece of wood, ¾ inch wide, ⅛ inch thick, approx. 6 inches long

# Putting on the Glitz

*Build a house for the glam birds in your home*

## WHAT YOU NEED

- 1 smooth wooden birdhouse
- 1 ½-pt/236-mL can Dynamic DynaPatch
- 180-grit sandpaper
- Dynamic Tack Cloth
- Dynamic 1-inch All Purpose Brush
- DecoArt Patio Paint:

   2 2-oz/59-mL bottles *Pot O' Gold*

   1 2-oz/59-mL bottle *Wrought Iron Black*
- craft jewels
- 40 mL bottle Elmer's Glue-All
- craft sparkles

## WHAT TO DO

1. Fill any small holes with DynaPatch. Lightly sand the wood. Wipe away dust, using the tack cloth. Apply 4 coats of *Pot O' Gold* paint, allowing to dry and lightly sanding between coats. Paint the base with 3 coats of *Wrought Iron Black* paint.

2. Glue craft jewels around the edge of the roof and opening.

3. Spread a thin layer of glue over the roof. Leave for 1 to 2 minutes, until the glue feels tacky. Sprinkle glitter on top, tapping to distribute it evenly.

**Note:** This birdhouse is for indoor decorative use only.

# Seating Plans

## Revitalize a rusted iron bench

### WHAT TO DO

1. Spread out the drop cloth in your work area, preferably outdoors. Use the wire brush to remove loose rust and paint from the bench.

2. Spread plastic, cut out from the drop cloth, over any parts of the bench you do not want to paint. Tape in place.

3. Following the manufacturer's instructions on the can, spray the metal with an even coat of *Deep Green* paint. Let dry, then spray lightly with a coat of *Mid Green* paint to create a verdigris finish. Remove the plastic and tape.

### WHAT YOU NEED

- Dynamic Plastic Drop Cloth
- Dynamic Brass Mini Wire Scratch Brush
- metal bench
- 1-inch KleenEdge Easy Mask Low-Tack Tape
- 1 340-g can Hammerite Anti-Rust Spray Paint, *Deep Green Hammered Finish*
- 1 340-g can Hammerite Anti-Rust Spray Paint, *Mid Green Hammered Finish*

**BEFORE**

# *Flower Power*

*Decorate flowerpots with wit and style*

## For a faux malachite look

### WHAT TO DO

1. Wet the Poly-Brush, then squeeze dry on paper towels. Apply a coat of *Wrought Iron Black* over the flowerpot, inside and out. Let dry.

2. Squirt out overlapping spirals of paint in the pie plate in the following order: *Dark Eucalyptus Green*, *Pine Green*, and *Light Eucalyptus Green*. Moisten the sea sponge, then squeeze dry in paper towels.

3. Dip the sponge into the paint, then press onto the outside of the pot. Create more paint spirals in the plate as required. Completely cover the pot with the green paints. Let dry.

### WHAT YOU NEED

- 1 6-inch/15.5-cm terra-cotta pot, clean and dry
- 1-inch Poly-Brush
- paper towels
- DecoArt Patio Paint: 1 2-oz/59-mL bottle each of *Wrought Iron Black*; *Dark Eucalyptus Green*; *Pine Green*; *Light Eucalyptus Green*
- aluminum pie plate
- Dynamic Sea Sponge, approximately 1 inch in diameter

# For a faux tortoise-shell look

## WHAT YOU NEED

- I 6-inch/15.5-cm terra-cotta pot, clean and dry
- I-inch Poly-Brush
- DecoArt Patio Paint: I 2-oz/59-mL bottle each of *Woodland Brown; Daisy Cream; Sunflower Yellow*
- DecoArt Americana Paint: I 2-oz/59-mL bottle each of *Raw Sienna; Burnt Sienna; Burnt Umber*
- Dynamic Craft Brush
- I old toothbrush
- I small saucer
- I small bottle rubbing alcohol
- hair dryer
- I 2-oz/59-mL bottle DecoArt Varnish (*satin*)

## WHAT TO DO

1. Wet the Poly-Brush, then squeeze dry on paper towels. Apply a coat of *Woodland Brown* over the flowerpot, inside and out. Let dry. If necessary, paint with a second coat.

2. Mix 2 parts *Daisy Cream* and 1 part *Sunflower Yellow* paint. Using the Poly-Brush, paint this mixture on the outside of the pot. Let dry.

3. Dilute *Raw Sienna* paint with an equal amount of water. Using the craft brush and this mixture, paint small sections of the pot, taking care that the paint does not run down the sides of the pot. As soon as the paint begins to dry, dip the toothbrush in rubbing alcohol and flick it over the drying paint. The paint will immediately pull away from the pot, revealing the color beneath.

4. Use the hair dryer to speed up the drying process, so that you can move on to another small section. When the sides are all painted, repeat the process on the rim and bottom of the pot. Let dry.

5. Repeat steps No. 3 and 4, using *Burnt Sienna* paint. Let dry, then repeat again, using *Burnt Umber* paint. Let dry.

6. Touch up the paint inside the pot, if necessary. Apply 2 or more coats of varnish to the outside of the pot, using the Poly-Brush.

# For a faux leopard-spot look

## WHAT TO DO

1. Wet the Poly-Brush, then squeeze dry on paper towels. Apply a coat of *Woodland Brown* over the flowerpot, inside and out. Let dry. If necessary, paint with a second coat.

2. Using the Poly-Brush, paint the outside of the pot with *Golden Honey*. Let dry.

3. Create *hairlike* brush strokes: using the craft brush and *Woodland Brown* paint, apply with a scratchy motion to create irregular spot and circle shapes on the pot.

4. Mix a little *Patio Brick* into the *Woodland Brown* paint and scratch-paint this inside the irregular circle shapes. Mix a little *Antique Mum* into the paints for lighter *hairs*. Add a little water to the paint to thin it, if desired. For the lightest *hair*, use a mixture of *Daisy Cream* and *Antique Mum* paint and apply using the Veining Brush. Let dry.

5. Use the Poly-Brush to apply 1 coat of *Clear Coat* to the outside of the pot.

## WHAT YOU NEED

- 1 6-inch/15.5-cm terra-cotta pot, clean and dry
- 1-inch Poly-Brush
- Dynamic Craft Brush
- Symphony Veining Brush
- DecoArt Patio Paint: 1 2-oz/59-mL bottle each of *Woodland Brown*; *Golden Honey*; *Patio Brick*; *Antique Mum*; *Daisy Cream*; *Clear Coat*

## WHAT YOU NEED

- wicker chair
- Dynamic Plastic Drop Cloth
- 1-inch KleenEdge Easy Mask Low-Tack Tape
- Crown Country Decorator Spray Paint:
  1 340-g can each of: *Fiddlers Green*; *Barn Brown*; *Egg Yolk*

# Wicker Wake-Up

## Spray-paint a wicker chair

### WHAT TO DO

1. Spread out the drop cloth in your work area, preferably outdoors. Tape plastic cut to fit from the drop cloth over the arms and the diamond or other pattern on the back of the chair. Spray the uncovered parts with *Fiddlers Green* paint. Let dry and apply a second coat. Let dry.

2. Tape plastic over the body of the chair and spray the arms with 2 coats of *Barn Brown* paint, allowing to dry between coats.

3. Tape plastic over the chair except for the diamond area and the rocker legs. Spray with 2 coats of *Egg Yolk* paint, allowing to dry between coats. Remove all the plastic and tape.

BEFORE

# Sitting Pretty

*Refresh resin chairs with a spiffy spray treatment*

## WHAT YOU NEED

- Dynamic Plastic Drop Cloth
- resin chairs
- 150-grit sandpaper
- Dynamic Tack Cloth
- 1 1-qt/946-mL can Flood ESP Easy Surface Prep
- clean cloths
- The Original CAN GUN Aerosol Spray Can Trigger-Handle (optional)
- 2 or more 340-g cans Hammerite Anti-Rust Spray Paint for each chair in the following colors: *Smooth Red; Light Blue; Dark Blue; Light Green; Yellow; Smooth Aluminum*

## WHAT TO DO

**Note:** Work outdoors or in a well ventilated area.

**1.** Spread out the drop cloth. (Do not use newspaper, as the ink may transfer to the painted surface.) Lightly sand the chairs to remove any rough edges. Wipe with the tack cloth. Wipe the chairs with a cloth moistened with ESP; wipe off with a clean cloth. Leave the chairs to *cure* for at least 90 minutes.

**2.** Attach the trigger handle to the spray can. Following the directions on the can, spray the chairs, each one a different color. Let dry, then spray again. Some colors require more than 2 coats. For extra durability, let the chairs sit for 4 to 6 weeks before use.

# $\mathcal{P}$roducts that make your projects look great

The shelves of do-it-yourself and hardware stores are overflowing with new products that make decorating fun for anyone with novel ideas, fantasy plans, keen interest and basic skills. New and improved tools, some of them disposable, complement the new products and tempt anyone who may be inspired to try a hand at exciting and innovative decorating projects. In most cases, the sales staff at these stores are well informed: they can help with technical information, while some can even help with artistic or design advice. Product labels are excellent and reliable sources of information: read them carefully before buying or starting a project.

## Great products for creating interior decorating projects

| **Product name:** | **Dazzling Metallics** |
|---|---|
| Manufacturer: | DecoArt |
| Uses: | An acrylic paint in bright, vibrant metallic colors for use on wood, tin, metal, resin, ceramics, papier-mâché, watercolor paper, Styrofoam and fabric. |
| How to apply: | Brush or sponge. |
| Cleanup: | Soap and water. |
| Special features: | Nontoxic; no heat setting required for painting on fabrics. |

| **Product name:** | **Royal Metallics** |
|---|---|
| Manufacturer: | DecoArt |
| Uses: | An acrylic paint that achieves an embossed foil, textured and metallic look in 1 step for use on wood, papier-mâché, plaster, resin, metal, glass and ceramic. |
| How to apply: | Brush or roller. |
| Cleanup: | Soap and water. |
| Special features: | Nontoxic; available in 4 metallic colors. |

**Product name:** **Brush 'n Blend Extender**
**Manufacturer:** DecoArt
**Uses:** An extender, which increases the drying time of paint; also facilitates blending of colors.
**How to apply:** Mix equal parts Brush 'n Blend with DecoArt Americana Acrylic paints
**Cleanup:** Soap and water.
**Special features:** Not for use with DecoArt Dazzling Metallics.

**Product name:** **Easy Blend Stencil Paint**
**Manufacturer:** DecoArt
**Uses:** To stencil shaded effects on walls, wood, fabric or paper.
**How to apply:** Stencil brush.
**Cleanup:** DecoArt Brush and Stencil Cleaner or dishwashing detergent and water.
**Special features:** Colors are intermixable; paint adheres to fabric with no heat setting required.

**Product name:** **Dynamic Metallic Leaf Finish Paint**
**Manufacturer:** Paint Sundry Products Inc.
**Uses:** Touch up decorative articles.
**How to apply:** Soft small brush.
**Cleanup:** Lacquer thinner.
**Special features:** Available in 4 shades of gold, silver, copper and antique; not recommended for exterior use.

**Product name:** **Dynamic Chalkboard Paint**
**Manufacturer:** Paint Sundry Products Inc.
**Uses:** Creates a blackboardlike surface.
**How to apply:** Bristle brush or Poly-Brush.
**Cleanup:** Mineral spirits.

**Product name:** **Tye-Tac**
**Manufacturer:** Tye-Sil Corp. Ltd.
**Uses:** Self-adhesive vinyl sheet.
**How to apply:** Peel off backing; press to surface.
**Special features:** Can be cut to fit any flat shape.

**Product name:** **Whizz Rollers**
**Manufacturer:** Paint Sundry Products Inc.
**Special features:** Available in many sizes, styles and materials for use in several situations.

**Product name:** **H₂O Acrylic Polyurethane Interior Finish**
**Manufacturer:** Old Masters
**Uses:** Protects interior wood surfaces, such as cabinets, doors, furniture, floors and tabletops.
**How to apply:** Polyester or foam brush, roller or spray.
**Cleanup:** Soap and water.
**Special features:** Nontoxic; environmentally friendly; dries fast; nonyellowing.

**Product name:** **Old Masters Poly Plastic Polyurethane**
**Manufacturer:** Old Masters
**Uses:** Protects interior wood surfaces, such as floors, bars, counters, doors.
**How to apply:** Pure-bristle or polyester brush, flat pad or spray.
**Cleanup:** Mineral spirits.
**Special features:** Nontoxic; not for use on linoleum, tile or over shellac or lacquer.

**Product name:** **Symphony Aged/Crackled Finishes – Top Coat and Base Coat Paint**
**Manufacturer:** Symphony Art, Inc.
**Uses:** Achieves a crackle finish on any porous unsealed surface using a base coat and top coat.
**How to apply:** Foam brush or sea sponge.
**Cleanup:** Soap and water.
**Special features:** Available in many colors and untinted.

**Product name:** **Projection Stenciling**
**Manufacturer:** Projection Stenciling
**Uses:** Projects any image onto a surface to be stenciled.
**How to apply:** Projector and freezer paper.
**Special features:** Kits and instructional video available.

**Product name:** **Decorplate**
**Manufacturer:** Paint Sundry Products Inc.
**Uses:** Clear plastic switch and/or electrical-plug plates produce decorative treatments.
**How to apply:** Sandwich wallpaper or fabric between the 2 layers; or paint lightweight cardboard with the same paint as on walls and sandwich between plastic.

**Product name:** **Blend & Glaze Decorative Painting Liquid (available in alkyd or latex)**
**Manufacturer:** Wm. Zinsser & Co., Inc.
**Uses:** Helps create decorative techniques, such as wood-graining, marbleizing,

granite, leather, antiquing, ragging, sponging, dragging and stenciling.

| | |
|---|---|
| How to apply: | Add to paints, following manufacturer's instructions. |
| Cleanup: | Soap and water. |

**Product name:** **Marble Ultra-Rich Base Coat and Marble Decorator Top Coat**

| | |
|---|---|
| Manufacturer: | Crown |
| Uses: | Creates a marbled look in 2 spray-on steps. |
| How to apply: | Spray. |
| Cleanup: | Soap and water while wet. |

**Product name:** **Ritins Studio Texture Roller**

| | |
|---|---|
| Manufacturer: | Ritins Studio Inc. |
| Uses: | To create textured appearance on walls. |
| How to apply: | Attach to roller cage; roll over glaze or wet paint. |
| Cleanup: | Depends on type of paint used. |

## Great products for creating exterior decorating projects

**Product name:** **Solid Color Deck & Siding Stain**

| | |
|---|---|
| Manufacturer: | The Flood Paint Specialty Co. Ltd. |
| Uses: | For use on exterior wood surfaces, including decks, siding, fences, trim boards, lattices, outdoor furniture and plywood. |
| How to apply: | Brush or roller. |
| Cleanup: | Soap and water. |
| Special features: | A combined primer and stain with a 5-year guarantee on decks, 15-year guarantee on siding; available in a wide variety of premixed, custom and traditional colors. |

**Product name:** **Dekswood Cleaner and Brightener for Exterior Wood**

| | |
|---|---|
| Manufacturer: | The Flood Paint Specialty Co. Ltd. |
| Uses: | Cleans and brightens exterior wood, such as decks, siding, fences, shake roofs. |
| How to apply: | Mix with water, as directed; work into the surface, using a stiff nylon or bristle brush; let stand for at least 30 minutes, then wash off with a garden hose or power washer. |
| Cleanup: | Water. |
| Special features: | Does not alter the inherent color of wood; takes out the grey and dirt, bringing the surface back to a rich |

new-wood look; cleans aluminum or vinyl siding, fiberglass and plastics.

**Product name:** **Perma-White Mildew-Proof Exterior Paint**

| | |
|---|---|
| Manufacturer: | Wm. Zinsser & Co., Inc. |
| Uses: | An acrylic water-based paint that beautifies, protects, resists fading, cracking and peeling. |
| How to apply: | Brush, roller or spray. |
| Cleanup: | Soap and water. |
| Special features: | Guaranteed to remain mildew-free for 5 years; has a bright white finish and can be custom-tinted to off-white or pastel shades; can be applied to previously painted or new surfaces, such as wood, cured concrete, stucco, stone, metals, vinyl, aluminum and hardboard siding; is not recommended for floors. |

## Great products for both interior and exterior use

**Product name:** **Americana Acrylic Paint**

| | |
|---|---|
| Manufacturer: | DecoArt |
| Uses: | An acrylic paint for use on wood, walls, metal, ceramic bisque, fabric, Styrofoam, canvas, paper and leather. |
| How to apply: | Brush on. |
| Cleanup: | Soap and water. |
| Special features: | Nontoxic; available in 181 colors, which may be mixed to create other colors. |

**Product name:** **Patio Paint**

| | |
|---|---|
| Manufacturer: | DecoArt |
| Uses: | An acrylic paint for painting, stenciling and faux finishes on concrete, masonry, stucco, terra-cotta, stone and wood, indoors and out. |
| How to apply: | Brush, sponge, stencil or roller . |
| Cleanup: | Soap and water. |
| Special features: | Weatherproof and durable in all weather conditions; nontoxic, scuff-resistant; available in 23 colors; prepacked kits available. |

**Product name:** **Country Decorator Spray Paint**

| | |
|---|---|
| Manufacturer: | Crown |
| Uses: | For use on metal, wood, wicker, ceramics, plastic, glass and craft foam, indoors and out. |

How to apply: Spray.
Cleanup: Soap and water.
Special features: Nontoxic; requires no primer.

**Product name: Ultra Gloss Air Dry Enamel**
Manufacturer: DecoArt
Uses: An acrylic gloss-finish paint to decorate glass, tile, prepared metals, terra-cotta, plaster, plastic, wood, vinyl and ceramic bisque with no baking requirements.
How to apply: Dry brush, stencil or sponge .
Cleanup: Soap and water.
Special features: Scratch-resistant; nontoxic; available in more than 30 colors; dishwasher-safe if baked 24 hours after painting at 325F for 30 minutes.

**Product name: Buckingham Stencils Inc. Water Based Acrylic Latex Paint**
Manufacturer: VeraDeco International Inc.
Uses: A water-based acrylic interior/exterior latex paint for stenciling on walls, furniture and floorcloths.
How to apply: Stencil brush or roller.
Cleanup: Soap and water.
Special features: Fast-drying; intermixable colors.

**Product name: DuraClear Exterior/Interior Varnish**
Manufacturer: DecoArt
Uses: A clear polyurethane varnish that adds a protective finish, indoors and out.
How to apply: Brush.
Cleanup: Soap and water.
Special features: Dries quickly; won't puddle or show brush strokes, is chemical- and water-resistant, so it won't show stains or rings left by wet glasses; nontoxic; nonyellowing.

**Product name: Sandstones Stonelike Textural Acrylics**
Manufacturer: DecoArt
Uses: A stonelike textural acrylic for interior and exterior use on walls, concrete, terra-cotta, wood, ceramic bisque, plaster, papier-mâché, resin, primed wrought iron or metal.
How to apply: Brush or roller.
Cleanup: Soap and water.
Special features: Available in 15 decorator colors;

weatherproof; nontoxic.

**Product name: Dynamic Water Based Acrylic Enamel**
Manufacturer: Paint Sundry Products Inc.
Uses: For interior or exterior use on metal, wood, Styrofoam, ceramics, glass, vinyl and most plastics.
How to apply: Spray.
Cleanup: Soap and water.
Special features: Water-resistant; dries quickly.

**Product name: Dynamic Enamel Paint**
Manufacturer: Paint Sundry Products Inc.
Uses: To touch up marred paint areas in high-gloss and flat finishes, indoors and out; may be applied to metal, wood, plastic, ceramic and most other surfaces.
How to apply: Brush.
Cleanup: Mineral spirits or paint thinner.
Special features: Nontoxic when dry; contains no lead.

**Product name: Hammerite Anti-Rust Paint**
Manufacturer: Hammerite
Uses: A long-lasting, self-priming high-gloss paint that stops and prevents rust in one step; can be applied over rusty, new or previously painted metal surfaces and on wood, plastic, fiberglass, stone and concrete.
How to apply: Brush, roller or spray.
Cleanup: Mineral spirits.
Special features: Fast-drying; available in 15 smooth colors and 14 hammered colors, including black and white; contains silicone; nonleaded; safe for children's toys.

**Product name: THICK 'n EZY Gel Stain**
Manufacturer: Old Masters
Uses: An oil-based gelled stain for use on wood, fiberglass, metal and composition surfaces.
How to apply: Brush or rag.
Cleanup: Paint thinner or mineral spirits.
Special features: Longer workable open time than other gel stains; will not leave lap marks or raise the grain of any woods.

**Product name: Buckingham Stencils**
Manufacturer: Buckingham Stencils Inc., under

license by VeraDeco International Inc.

**Uses:** To stencil designs on flat surfaces.

**How to apply:** Tape on surface or spray underside of stencil with repositionable stencil spray and press onto surface; then apply paint with brush or roller.

**Cleanup:** Wipe clean, using medium used to clean brushes.

**Special features:** Stencils are laser-cut from durable 7-mL Mylar, making them suitable for repeated use.

**Product name:** **Blue Mountain Stencils**

**Manufacturer:** Blue Mountain Stencil Co.

**Uses:** To stencil designs on flat surfaces

**How to apply:** Tape on surface or spray underside of stencil with repositionable stencil spray and press onto surface, then apply paint with brush or roller.

**Cleanup:** Wipe clean, using medium used to clean brushes.

**Special features:** Stencils are cut from 5-mL Mylar with register marks on all sheets for ease in repositioning; patterns were created by wildlife artist Marten Visser.

**Product name:** **Decor Stamps**

**Manufacturer:** Paint Designs

**Uses:** A system of rubber-stamp designs for use with acrylic paints in decorating walls, floors, fabrics and other flat surfaces.

**How to apply:** Attach rubber-stamp design to plastic holder; use a foam roller to apply latex paint to stamp, then press onto surface.

**Cleanup:** Soap and water.

**Special features:** 28 patterns available.

**Product name:** **The Cutbill Block Printing System**

**Manufacturer:** Paint Sundry Products Inc.

**Uses:** Decorative accents for walls, floors and furniture.

**How to apply:** Apply Cutbill latex glaze to precut block printing pads; press onto surface.

**Cleanup:** Soap and water.

**Special Features:** 32 patterns and 28 glaze colors available.

**Product name:** **Repositionable Stencil Adhesive Spray**

**Manufacturer:** Blue Mountain Stencil Co.

**Uses:** Temporarily adheres stencils to any surface.

**How to apply:** Spray to underside of stencil.

**Special features:** Repositionable.

**Product name:** **Buckingham Stencil Adhesive Spray**

**Manufacturer:** Buckingham Stencils Inc., under license by VeraDeco International Inc.

**Uses:** Temporarily adheres stencils to any surface.

**How to apply:** Spray to underside of stencil.

**Special features:** Repositionable.

## Other handy helpful products

**Product name:** **Dynamic Plastic Drop Cloth**

**Manufacturer:** Paint Sundry Products Inc.

**Uses:** Protects surrounding surfaces from painting or stripping projects.

**Special features:** Available in 3 weights, size 9 feet x 12 feet.

**Product name:** **Dynamic Tack Cloth**

**Manufacturer:** Paint Sundry Products Inc.

**Uses:** Picks up all dirt, dust and sanding residue during painting, refinishing furniture and floors, craftwork and hobbies.

**Special features:** Antistatic.

**Product name:** **Dynamic Fine Quality Painting and Stripping Gloves and Dynamic All Purpose Disposable Latex Gloves**

**Manufacturer:** Paint Sundry Products Inc.

**Uses:** Keep hands clean and odor-free during decorating projects and protect hands from products that may irritate skin.

**Special features:** Fit either hand; reusable but economical enough to throw away.

**Product name:** **Gloves in a Bottle**

**Manufacturer:** Paint Sundry Products Inc.

**Uses:** Prevents most irritants, toxins, dirt, paint, grease and detergents from penetrating the skin for up to 4 hours.

**How to apply:** Like hand lotion.

**Special features:** Does not wash off; softens the skin.

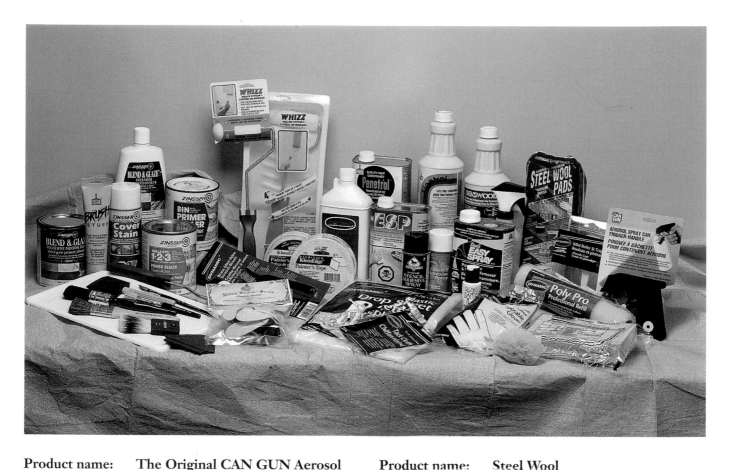

**Product name:** **The Original CAN GUN Aerosol Spray Can Trigger-Handle**
**Manufacturer:** SafeWorld International Inc.
**Uses:** Improves spray action of aerosol paints, lubricants, adhesives and cleaners.

**Product name:** **KleenEdge High-Tack Painter's Tape**
**Manufacturer:** DCP-Lojha Inc.
**Uses:** To mark or mask off areas on all surfaces, inside and out.
**How to apply:** Press firmly in place.
**Special features:** Removes easily with no adhesive residue; no paint bleed-through; no seepage when pressed firmly to smooth surfaces ; available in 4 widths.

**Product name:** **KleenEdge Easy Release Painter's Tape**
**Manufacturer:** DCP-Lojha Inc.
**Uses:** To mark or mask off areas on all surfaces, inside and out.
**How to apply:** Press firmly in place.
**Special features:** Removes easily with no adhesive residue; available in 4 widths.

**Product name:** **Steel Wool**
**Manufacturer:** Rhodes American
**Uses:** Removes old finishes in conjunction with strippers without damaging the surface; cleans and removes rust from metal surfaces; restores brass, copper and bronze.
**Special features:** Economical and environmentally degradable; available in 8 grades.

**Product name:** **Elmer's Glue-All**
**Manufacturer:** The Borden Co. Ltd.
**Uses:** For gluing porous material, such as wood, leather and cloth.
**Cleanup:** Water.
**Special features:** Dries clear; is not damaged by freezing.

**Product name:** **ESP Easy Surface Prep**
**Manufacturer:** The Flood Paint Specialty Co. Ltd.
**Uses:** Cleans old surfaces, such as varnished or enameled woodwork, prefinished paneling and furniture, baked enameled appliances, glass and ceramic tile; leaves a permanent bonding film to provide adhesion for oil/alkyd or latex paints.

How to use: Brush, roller or rag.

Cleanup: Mineral spirits or paint thinner.

Special features: Eliminates the need for sanding; does not soften or harm old finishes; mild odor and easy on the hands.

**Product name:** Bulls Eye 1-2-3 Primer/Sealer

Manufacturer: Wm. Zinsser & Co., Inc.

Uses: A water-based primer/sealer for use under oil-based or water-based top coats, inside or outside. It adheres to laminates, ceramic tiles, galvanized metal, aluminum, gloss paints and enamels; it kills most stains and rust damage and seals all porous surfaces, such as cured masonry, stucco and brick.

How to apply: Brush, roller, pad or spray.

Cleanup: Soap and water.

Special features: Odorless, dries in 1 hour.

**Product name:** B-I-N White Pigmented Shellac Primer/Sealer

Manufacturer: William Zinsser & Co., Inc.

Uses: A quick-drying interior undercoat that primes, seals and kills stains, all in one coat. It can be used on drywall, plaster, new wood, wallpapered surfaces, wallboard, plywood, glass, glossy surfaces, metal, laminates and ceramic tile.

How to apply: Roller, brush, pad or spray.

Cleanup: Household ammonia solution, denatured alcohol, or Methyl Hydrate.

Special features: Dries in 45 minutes; forms a vapor barrier on interior walls; adheres to glossy surfaces; kills smoke stains and odors.

**Product name:** Cover Stain Primer/Sealer

Manufacturer: Wm. Zinsser & Co., Inc.

Uses: A primer/sealer, stain-killer and bond coat, for interior and exterior uses on wood, wallboard, tiles, glass and painted surfaces. It covers graffiti, nicotine and water stains. As a bonding primer, it prepares glossy surfaces for painting. It is not recommended for galvanized metal or some plaster.

How to apply: Spray or brush.

Cleanup: Mineral spirits or paint thinner.

Special features: Available in both aerosol and liquid form.

**Product name:** Penetrol

Manufacturer: The Flood Paint Specialty Co. Ltd.

Uses: A durable paint oil used either alone or as a treatment coating for metal or wood; also used as a paint additive to assure smooth and easy application of varnish, oil- or asphalt-base paints.

How to apply: Brush.

Cleanup: Mineral spirits or paint thinner.

Special features: Slows the drying process of paints, thus increasing open working time; increases the working time of glazes; inhibits the spread of rust.

**Product name:** Floetrol

Manufacturer: The Flood Paint Specialty Co. Ltd.

Uses: Extends water-based paints and improves application to surfaces, reduces tip clogging in sprayers; provides a spraylike finish.

How to apply: Brush, roller or spray.

Cleanup: Soap and water.

Special features: Eliminates lapping, streaking and shadowing problems in paint applications; increases the working time of glazes; slows the drying time of paints.

**Product name:** Dad's Easy Spray Paint, Stain & Varnish Remover

Manufacturer: Sansher Corp.

Uses: Removes paint, varnish, lacquer, shellac, stains, latex, acrylic and polyurethane from furniture, woodwork, floors and masonry without harming patina or wood grains.

How to apply: Spray.

Cleanup: Solvent.

Special features: Fast-acting.

**Product name:** Dynamic Paint Thinner/Mineral Spirits

Manufacturer: Paint Sundry Products Inc.

Uses: Thins oil-based paints, cleans brushes and rollers, removes dirt and wax from hardwood, linoleum, vinyl and terrazzo floors, removes grease, oil, tar and wax from aluminum doors, ceramic or plastic tiles and concrete; removes grease, tar or oily stains from fabrics and carpets.

How to apply: Rag.

Special Features: Ensure used rags are completely dry before throwing them out.

**Product name:** **Poly-Brush**
Manufacturer: Poly-Brush
Uses: For applying all paints, stains, varnishes and urethanes to smooth surfaces; not for use with shellac or lacquer.
Special features: Available in several widths; washable; economical enough to discard after use.

**Product name:** **Dynamic brushes and rollers**
Manufacturer: Paint Sundry Products Inc.
Uses: Available in many sizes, styles and materials for several uses.

**Product name:** **Dynamic Brass Mini Wire Scratch Brush**
Manufacturer: Paint Sundry Products Inc.
Uses: For stripping varnish or paint from hard-to-reach areas.
Special features: Removes rust, grime and mildew.

**Product name:** **Grey Goat Hair Brush**
Manufacturer: Symphony Art, Inc.
Uses: For softening and blending glazes or washing out colors when faux-finishing.

**Product name:** **Badger Blender**
Manufacturer: Symphony Art, Inc.
Uses: A brush for softening and blending glazes when applying faux-finishing techniques.

**Product name:** **Veining Brush**
Manufacturer: Symphony Art, Inc.
Uses: Also known as a Sable Dagger, it is used to create fine lines or broad strokes for faux-finishing.

**Product name:** **Triangular Graining Comb**
Manufacturer: Symphony Art, Inc.
Uses: Creates three different patterns when faux-graining.

**Product name:** **Buckingham Stencil Roller and Tray**
Manufacturer: Buckingham Stencils Inc., under license by VeraDeco International Inc.
Uses: For applying paints to stencils.

**Product name:** **Buckingham Stencil Brush**
Manufacturer: Buckingham Stencils Inc., under license by VeraDeco International Inc.
Uses: Applies paint to stencils.

**Product name:** **Portofino Marble Faux Finishing Starter Tool Set**
Manufacturer: Symphony Art, Inc.
Uses: Prepackaged tools and instructions to create a faux marble finish.

**Product name:** **Dynamic All Metal Junior Snap-Off Cutter**
Manufacturer: Paint Sundry Products Inc.
Uses: For cutting paper, cardboard, leather, vinyl and more.
Special features: Blunt used end snaps off to provide new sharp surface for cutting.

**Product name:** **Dynamic Sea Sponge and Cellulose Sponge**
Manufacturer: Paint Sundry Products Inc.
Uses: For creating faux finishes and applying small amounts of paint.

# Sources

**Renaissance revival**
Suzanne Davison Designs Inc.

**Cabinet secrets**
*Bowl, candlesticks,* B. B. Bargoon's; *all other accessories,* Suzanne Davison Designs Inc.

**Clever headboard**
*Pillows, bedding, throw, clock, bowl, magazine rack, dog, print,* Elte Carpets & Home; *candle, curtains,* B. B. Bargoon's.

**Animal instincts**
*Accessories, table mirror, towels,* Ginger's International Bath Centre; *prints,* B. B. Bargoon's

**Faux-finished fantasy**
*Bath accessories and towels,* Ginger's International Bath Centre.

**Stripe it rich**
*Letter box, cigar box, candles, magazine rack, print,* Elte Carpets & Home.

**Top drawer!**
*Letter holder, pencil holder,* Elte Carpets & Home.

**Perky picnic table**
*Napkins, napkin rings, glasses,* Jacaranda Tree; *dinnerware,* Bowring.

**Hit the deck**
*Cushions,* B. B. Bargoon's.

**Metal urges**
*Chair-seat fabric, napkins, purse,* En Provence; *all other accessories,* Suzanne Davison Designs Inc.


The *trays* on page 1 (Mumby logo) and page 37 were created by Linda Buckingham of Buckingham Stencils.
The *drop-front desk,* on page 10, *filing cabinet* on page 35 and the *faux-marble vanity doors* on page 28 were created by Kelly Smirl of Decorative Finishes, 416/656-0118.
The *blackboard divider screen* on page 19, the *leopard-spot mirror frame* on page 25, the *leopard-spot lampshade* on page 30 and the *birdhouses* on pages 59, 61, and 62 were created by Chris Brooks, 905/372-1636.
The *tray* on page 36, and *padded mirror frame,* page 16, were created by Moya McPhail, 416/489-7738
The *birdbath* on page 56 was created by Sharyn Adler Gitalis of Creative Painted Environments, 416/250-1249.
The *flowerpots* on pages 65, 66 and 67 were created by Barbara Kerr, Decorative Artist and Custom Design Studio, 905/469-9455.


B. B. Bargoon's, 1-800-665-9227
Bowring, stores across Canada
Elte Carpets & Home, 416/785-7885
En Provence, 416/975-7400
Ginger's International Bath Centre, 416/787-7887
Jacaranda Tree, 416/482-6599
Suzanne Davison Designs Inc., 416/481-5254

# Index